THE MESSAGE OF ISRAEL

Sermons   Addresses   Memoirs

BY THE SAME AUTHOR:

The Jewish Law of Agency—With Special Reference to the Roman and Common Law

Steering or Drifting—Which?

Judaism—An Analysis and an Interpretation

A New World is Born

Judaism Speaks to the Modern World

Point of View—An Analysis of American Judaism

Song and Praise for Sabbath Eve (with Rabbi Israel Goldfarb)

TRANSLATIONS OF THE AUTHOR'S WORKS:

Hayahadut V'haolam Hamodarni (A Hebrew translation of Selected Sermons) by Rabbi Hyman Rabinowitz, in Israel.

Judentum (A Yiddish translation of Judaism—an Analysis and an Interpretation) by Dr. Abraham Asen.

THE MESSAGE OF ISRAEL

Sermons   Addresses   Memoirs

BY

ISRAEL H. LEVINTHAL

Rabbi of The Brooklyn Jewish Center

LEX PRINTING COMPANY, INC.
NEW YORK
1973

TABLE OF CONTENTS

INTRODUCTION

In the Introductions of several of my previously published works, I had occasion to express what I believe to be the function of the Jewish sermon. It is appropriate to repeat here my firm conviction that the Jewish sermon, while discussing all problems involving modern life—those specifically Jewish and those of a general or universal nature—must be based upon the teachings and interpretations of our classic Jewish literature.[1] Unless it has such foundation, it is not a true Jewish sermon—even though delivered from a Synagogue pulpit—and has no greater Jewish authenticity than an address given by a layman.

At this period of my life, I may be pardoned if, putting aside modesty, I state unequivocally that I do not recall a sermon or address of mine—including any spoken at a secular or even Christian gathering —which was not connected with or did not seek to present a new insight or interpretation of a Biblical or Rabbinic text.

The sermons in this volume were selected because of their relevance to important issues confronting the Jew today. Because of a desire to limit this book to a handy size, I have omitted many other sermons which are pertinent.

Some of the High Holy Day sermons have already been published in the Brooklyn Jewish Center Review, a periodical now appearing annually. All the Festival and Hanukkah sermons here are set forth

---

1. For a more detailed treatment of this subject see my article, "The Uniqueness of the Classic Jewish Sermon", in *Conservative Judaism,* Winter Issue, March, 1973.

i

in print for the first time. They are based on short notes or outlines which I used when I delivered them from the pulpit. I have endeavored to keep all sermons brief, omitting the elaborations which were essential or apt at the time of preaching.

The address delivered at the Second Convention of the Brooklyn Jewish Community Council in 1954 has not been printed previously. I believe that, even though presented years ago, when the Brooklyn Council was a pioneer in that type of organization, it is particularly relevant today because it offers a guiding principle which should concern the many Community Councils being currently established.

The address, "On Serving Fifty Years in the Rabbinate," was part of the Proceedings of the Rabbinical Assembly Convention in 1964. Since it may be of interest to a larger sphere of readers, it is, with the permission of the Editors of the Proceedings, reprinted here.

My tribute to my wife, May, of blessed memory, was published as a pamphlet immediately after its delivery at the Brooklyn Jewish Center. Because of wide requests for its publication in permanent form, it is included in this volume.

My Memoirs and Reminiscences appeared in the October, 1955 and September to December, 1956 issues of the Brooklyn Jewish Center Review, shortly after the celebration of the 35th anniversary of my Rabbinate at the Center. Their portrayal of early Jewish life in an important American city and of fascinating personalities whom I had been privileged to meet at the home of my illustrious father, Rabbi

Bernard L. Levinthal, of blessed memory, one of the outstanding leaders of the orthodox Jewish community of America, has evoked continuing interest in their republication. Accordingly, it was deemed fitting to include them in this permanent collection.

* * *

I acknowledge specially my indebtedness to the brothers, Mr. Moe Mark and Mr. Louis Mark, for their generosity in having this volume published in conjunction with the celebration by the Brooklyn Jewish Center of my eighty-fifth birthday.

My relationship with these dear friends goes back to the years 1915-1919, when I was the Rabbi of Temple Petach Tikvah in Brooklyn. Their parents, Harry and Mamie Mark (Zvi Mordechai ben R. Shmuel and Michka bas R. Zvi Hirsh), of blessed memory, had been among the founding members of the Temple. Moe and Louis Mark have for years been ardent supporters of the Brooklyn Jewish Center, and Moe has rendered distinguished service as a member of its Board of Trustees.

I pray that they may be blessed "with the dew of heaven and the substance of the earth" so as to be able to continue their fruitful service in the vineyard of Israel for many years to come.

I express my gratitude to my son-in-law, Mr. Lester Lyons, of the New York Bar, for his kindness in reading the manuscript and for his many helpful suggestions by which this work has profited. My thanks are conveyed to Mrs. Dorothy Rose, of the Brooklyn Jewish Center staff, for her favor in typing most of the material in this volume.

iii

Above all, in entering my eighty-sixth year I recall with love and gratefulness my cherished and devoted helpmate, May R. Levinthal, who shared with me fifty-eight years of deep happiness and whose inspiration is still the guiding force in my life.

ISRAEL H. LEVINTHAL

Shevat 12, 5733   February 12, 1973

THE TWO NEW YEARS OF THE JEW*

We Jews are a singular people—we can truly say: "And who is like unto Thy people, Israel, a unique people on earth".[1] We are the only people who celebrate two New Years. In fact, the Talmud speaks of four New Years which the ancient Jews observed;[2] but we still mark two principal New Years.

Reckoning in years, we have Rosh Hashanah. Yesterday was still 5730; today is the first day of the year 5731. But, reckoning in months, we have another New Year, beginning with the month of Nissan. Tishre, the month of Rosh Hashanah, is not the first month in our calendar; it is the seventh month. The Bible, in enjoining the observance of Rosh Hashanah, specifically states: "And in the seventh month, on the first day of the month, ye shall have a holy convocation . . . it is a day of blowing the shofar unto you."[3] On the other hand, in the calendar of the months, the Bible, in speaking of Nissan, the month marking the event of Passover, states: "This month shall be for you the beginning of the months . . . it is the first of the months of the year."[4]

In the registers of all other people, January is both the first month of the year and the beginning of

---

* Rosh Hashanah, 1970.
1. I Chronicles, 17:21.
2. Mishnah, Rosh Hashanah, 1:1.
3. Leviticus 22:14; Deut., 29:1.
4. Exodus, 12:2.

the new calendar year. We Jews alone have a special New Year for the yearly calendar as well as for the monthly calendar. Each of these New Years has a distinctive meaning and function.

Tishre, the month of Rosh Hashanah, marks the creation of the world: "This day the world came into being." Nay, more—it was in the beginning of Tishre that the first man—Adam—was created; not the first Jew, but the first *man*, the ancestor of all human beings on earth.[5] Nissan, the New Year of the months, commemorates the birth of the Jewish people, their redemption from Egypt, and the beginning of their peoplehood.

Look at the history of other ancient nations; it begins with the origin of their own people. For example, the history of Rome starts with the story of Romulus, the founder of that city. Not so with the Jew. Take our Bible—it does not begin with Moses and the deliverance of our people, nor even with Abraham, the founder of our faith and the progenitor of our people. It starts with the history of *Man*—universal man.

Rashi, the greatest of our commentators, marks this striking fact. On the very first verse of the Bible, he notes: "The Bible should really have begun with the twelfth chapter of Exodus, 'This month shall be for *you* the first of the month,' which tells the story of Israel's redemption and the birth of its peoplehood. But it begins with the story of the creation of the world and the first human being, to teach us that *kol haaretz shel Hakadosh baruch Hu*—the whole earth belongs to God," and that all mankind is His concern.

---

5. Leviticus Rabbah, 29:1.

Herein is revealed the genius of the Jew. We celebrate both New Years—the birth of universal Man, and also the birth of our own, the Jewish, people. Both are of our deepest concern! We think of ourselves—our own people—but not only of ourselves. We think of all mankind!

And this represents the ideal of the Jew throughout the ages. He thought, he prayed, he worked for the welfare of all mankind. Ernest Renan, the great French thinker, termed the Hebrew prophets "the first true socialists." They pleaded to and for the Jew; but theirs was also a universal message—a plea for universal justice, righteousness and peace.

The tragedy of the world today is that nations have not learned the need for these two New Years. Each country observes the message of "This month shall be *for you*," but is not concerned with the rest of the world, except in so far as that concern affects its own national interest.

Lewis Mumford, the brilliant author, did not realize that he was expressing a truth which the Jew had proclaimed at the beginning of his history, when he said: "He who is 100% American, or 100% Russian, is only half a man. The universal part of his personality, equally essential to becoming human, is still unborn."

Just as we note the tragedy of the nations of the world, so, too, we note a new tragedy in the life of the Jews. We see many Jewish youth—alas, too many—who observe the universal message of Tishre —interested in and working for all the world—but who have forsaken the message of Nissan—to remember to work *lachem* "for you," for their own people, and to help preserve them, particularly in these days when millions of enemies want to put an end to their existence.

For Jews to work for and in behalf of the deprived Negro, or the downtrodden and poverty-stricken in America, or for the poor and disfranchised of the world, is all to the good and within the Jewish tradition. But this is only half their duty. There is a second half of their duty—equally important—to work for their own people. Alas, how this part has been neglected! We have reached the tragic state of seeing a number of our youth aligned with our enemies, even soliciting funds for the Al Fatah and joining them in their determination to extinguish our national life in Israel.

When a Jew writes a novel—unfortunately so popular among Jewish readers—in which he complains to his psychiatrist about his parents, I can overlook the filth and the obscenities which abound in it; for, after all, they are the sensational stock in trade today to lure readers. But I cannot forgive him when he complains about his mother that she kept drilling into his ears: "Jew, Jew, Jew! It is coming out of my ears already, the saga of the suffering Jew! I also am a human being."

Here, he libels not only his mother but also the Jewish people. If anyone was a human being in addition to being true to his people, it was the Jew! If his mother kept drilling the words Jew, Jew, Jew into his ears, it was because she knew that he would manifest his humanity as a result of his intrinsic Jewish heritage. Moreover, wise mother that she was, she also knew that it was necessary through such means to help counteract the worldly influences that would envelop him and seek to make him forget his duties to his own people, especially today when the Jews in Israel are threatened with annihilation, and when our brethren in Russia face spiritual genocide.

And so this Rosh Hashanah has a message for the nations of the world: Cease being egocentric! Think of yourself but also beyond yourself! Give thought to the welfare of all nations and all peoples of the world!

And to the Jew, Rosh Hashanah pleads: It is good to work for the welfare of those in need among all the peoples in the world, to remember the universal message of this day. But that is only half of your duty; you have a second New Year—the month of Nissan—and it behooves you to remember its message, as well—your duty to yourself and to the people of which you are part!

There is an interesting discussion among the Rabbis of the Talmud:[6] "When will the *geulah*—the redemption—come?" Rabbi Eliezer answered: "In the month of Tishre." Rabbi Joshua said: "In the month of Nissan." When there is no declaratory decision, we may assume that both are correct. When the Jew and all the nations will learn to unite the messages of the two New Years, which symbolize the redemption of themselves and of the world, then will the true *geulah* appear—the glorious day when the Kingdom of Heaven will reign on earth!

---

6. Rosh Hashanah, 11b.

BROTHERS OR COMRADES?*

All of you are acquainted with the custom which we Jews observe, of ushering in the new month with a special prayer on the Sabbath preceding *Rosh Chodesh.* There is only one month in the year which is not ushered in with such a prayer, and that is the month of Tishre. The Rabbis in the Talmud[1] discuss this exception and offer explanation for it. We can understand the reason: the month of *Tishre* marks not only a new month but also the beginning of a new year; and in the liturgy of Rosh Hashanah we pray for the blessings which we so fervently want and need, for the entire year as well as for the month.

The prayers on that special Sabbath consist of three or four paragraphs. The first is an individual prayer, in which each of us asks our Heavenly Father for the blessings of long life, health, bodily vigor, love of Torah and reverence of God—a month in which all the desires of our hearts shall be realized.

The second paragraph concentrates on our concern for the entire people of Israel. We think of their present plight and pray: "May He who wrought wondrous deeds for our ancestors, and delivered them from slavery to freedom, grant a speedy redemption unto us, and may He gather our exiles from the four corners of the earth." And we then conclude with the inspiring phrase, *chaverim kol*

---

* Rosh Hashanah, 1967.
1. cf. Erubin, 40a; Hebrew Encyclopedia, IV, pp. 451-453.

[7]

Yisrael, "all Israelites are comrades; and let us say, Amen."

I want to pause and consider with you particularly this concluding phrase. The words *"chaverim kol Yisrael"* seem to have no connection whatsoever with what precedes them. They appear to be superfluous. The words "and let us say, Amen" could well have come after our preceding plea.

It is interesting to observe that scholars who specialize in Liturgy—the study of our Prayer Book —have been puzzled by this insertion, and some of them offer interesting interpretations.

Whatever may be the scholarly explanation for the appearance of this phrase, I have a deeper question: Why did the author of the prayer use the word *"chaverim"*? Should he not rather have used the term *"Achim kol Yisrael"*? "All Israelites are brothers"? After all, it would seem that *achim* (brothers) is a stronger word to be used than *chaverim* (comrades). We all pride ourselves on being the children of the same patriarchs, Abraham, Isaac and Jacob. As the brothers said to Joseph, "We are all children of one father" [2]; and *achim* (brothers) would emphasize that thought much more emphatically than *chaverim* (comrades).

And yet, upon deeper consideration, we find that our author had a good reason, and used fine judgment, in choosing the word *"chaverim"*—comrades —instead of *"achim"*—brothers. He had a deliberate purpose in adopting the phrase *chaverim kol Yisrael,* "all Israelites are comrades."

---

2. Genesis, 42:11.

There is a great difference between an *"ach"*, brother, and a *"chaver"*, comrade. We do not choose a brother—he is born to our family; we choose a comrade. The one is an accident of birth; the other is the result of deliberate choice. You and I have seen many cases in which brothers have no interest in each other and have no concern for each other; only in time of trouble or tragedy may the feeling of brotherliness awaken—and then, perhaps merely momentarily. A comrade or friend is at your side at all times, and his concern for you and interest in you are shown not only in time of sorrow but also in joyous or ordinary times. The wise author of Proverbs emphasizes this thought when he tells us: "A friend loveth at all times; a brother is born *l'tzarah*, in adversity." [3]

My friends, we saw this truth exemplified in recent days in the life of our people. During the few weeks of the Arab mobilization of their armies at the borders of Israel, and especially during the six days war in June, we witnessed a remarkable outpouring of sympathy and support for Israel by thousands of American Jews who, before those trying days, had shown no concern for Israel—indeed, who had had no interest in any phase of Jewish life —religious or cultural. They had been completely alienated from, or, at best, had been apathetic to, all Jewish life. But, suddenly, *"b'et tzarah"*, in a time of adversity or tragedy, the dormant feeling of brotherliness was awakened, and they responded magnificently to Israel's needs.

The same was true in 1947 and 1948, in connection with the War for Israel's Independence, as to

---

3. Proverbs, 17:17.

Jews who had had absolutely no interest, and who
had wanted no part, in Jewish life—Jews who were
completely assimilated. Suddenly, *"v'ach l'tzarah
yivaled"*—the hidden spark of brotherliness was
kindled—and they arose to help, to work, and, even
in some cases, to fight for Israel, in her bitter
struggle.

Alas, however, after the War of Independence,
when things became normal and Israel was no longer
in danger, this awakened feeling of brotherliness on
the part of many of them became dormant again.

The intellectual leaders of our people today, both
in Israel and in America, are deeply concerned about
what will happen to this feeling of brotherliness that
we have witnessed in the hearts of many previously
disinterested Jews: will these persons return to their
indifference and apathy when the danger facing
Israel is past—or will they be transformed from
achim to *chaverim*, from brothers to comrades, so
that we may be able to say of each of them, "at all
times the friend loveth!"?

This is the challenge that faces us American Jews
today: How can we change these *achim* into
chaverim?

What makes one choose another for a friend? Why
does A choose B and not another for his companion?
The answer is simple: A sees in B the qualities of
personality, of thinking, that he admires—qualities
which respond to his own needs; and thus he is
happy to enjoy his comradeship.

And that is exactly what we have to do to make
the *achim* want to be *chaverim* to the Jewish people.
We have to make them see the beauties of the true

Jewish life, the relevance of the ideals and teachings of our people's prophets and sages to their own spiritual needs. Once they will see these things and get to know them, they will desire to be *chaverim* to our people.

Our great tragedy is that we have failed to bring this knowledge to them. True, more children attend Hebrew School today than in previous years; but of what value is this instruction, if, as is the case with the large majority of our youth, Jewish studies are not continued by the boy who has become Bar Mitzvah or by the girl who has been confirmed or consecrated? In the most important years of their adolescence, when their minds are maturing, when they could get a ripe understanding of the vital teachings of Judaism for our day, they leave their Jewish studies—and thus they either forget what they had learned, or, at best, remain with childish notions of Jewish beliefs and ideals. Is it so strange then that, when these young people enter college and face the new philosophies and sciences of our time, they become quickly alienated from the precious heritage of their own people?

Maimonides, it seems to me, has epitomized the answer to our problem when he tells us: "*Talmide chachamim*, students of the wise, are called *chaverim*." [4] In the days of Maimonides, and for many years thereafter, scholars and even wise students of the Torah were given the honored title of *chaver*. Only those who are students of our Torah can be called *chaverim*. And Maimonides goes further and gives us the reason for his statement: "And the

---

4. Perush Hamishnah, Dmai, 2:3.

reason they are called by this title is that their fellowship and comradeship one towards the other, is a *chaverah ne'emanah*, a genuine and faithful fellowship." [5] Now, especially, when we are witnessing the fulfillment of the prayer, "May He redeem us and may He gather our exiles from the four corners of the earth," now, when we have been privileged to see how these ingathered Jews fought so bravely to defend their land and their people, now, when so many of our newly awakened Jews have felt the spark of *achavah*, now, it is our great opportunity to transform these *achim* (brothers) into *chaverim* (comrades), unto a *chaverah ne'emanah*, a true and faithful comradeship.

The Rabbis translate the Psalmist's words, "Jerusalem that is now rebuilt, a city bound together",[6] to mean, "It is the city that maketh all Israel into *chaverim*, into a fellowship." [7]

Now that Jerusalem is united into its old glory, we have the opportunity to fulfill the Rabbis' faith and hope that the rebuilt and reunited Jerusalem shall be the city *"schemachberet yisrael zeh lazeh,* that will unite in comradeship every Jew to his fellow Jew," [8] so that we will be able to say with pride and with happiness, *"Chaverim kol Yisrael,* all Israelites are comrades!"

---

5. Ibid.
6. Psalms, 122:3.
7. Jerusalem Talmud, Chagigah, 3:6. Midrash Psalms, 122:4.
8. Jer. Baba Kama, 7:10.

THE DEEPER MEANING OF THE
REVOLTS IN OUR DAY*

One of the great figures in our history was the spiritual head of the Academy of Sura in Babylon, in the tenth century, Rabbenu Saadya Gaon. He was a man of many achievements—author of the first Hebrew grammar, of rabbinic commentaries, of a great philosophic work, *Emunot V'deot*, "Faith and Knowledge", and a translator of the Bible into Arabic.

In reading a scholarly study of this Arabic translation, I was struck by the writer's statement that the word *vayomer*, wherever it appears in the first chapter in Genesis, is translated by Saadya not as we find it in all other translations—and as we usually translate it—"And He said," but as "And He *willed*." Thus, in place of the customary translation, "God *said*, Let there be light," Saadya stated, "God *willed* that there be light, and there was light." And similarly in the other passages dealing with the act of creation.

I believe that Saadya Gaon, being a philosopher as well as a translator, intended to include in this translation a fine philosophic truth, namely that even the Holy One Blessed Be He, *Kaviyochol* (as we would say) would not attempt to fashion a cosmos out of chaos by the mere power of words, but only by the process of *Will*, of determination. When there is *Will*, all else is possible.

---

* Rosh Hashanah, 1969.

We are living in an age of revolution. In every aspect of life we are facing revolt. What is the deeper meaning of this phenomenon? I think Saadya offers us an explanation.

For ages, man knew that the world was beset with evil. Philosophers and scientists wrote and talked about this problem, suggesting solutions for its eradication. And mankind was patient, hoping that their words—written and spoken—would bring salvation—but in vain! Today, men realize that speech alone will be of no avail. Instead of being content with *vayomer*, with words, they are beginning to show a *Will* for change. And already we see how fast *Will* is producing change.

Let me give a few brief examples. For over a century great thinkers—philosophers, sociologists, psychologists—offered panaceas for the evils of racism, which denied millions of our black brethren the ordinary rights of human beings or American citizens. And for a century the black man was patient, hoping that all such words would favorably affect the American mind and heart. Today, he is fed up with talk and shows a determined *Will* for change. We see that more changes have been effected in the last fifteen or twenty years than in the entire century before.

True, fault may be found with the methods used by some of the extremists among the blacks and their white sympathizers. Our Rabbis of old could have taught these extremists a valuable lesson. Even God did not manifest *Will* alone. Before creating the world, He created the Torah—the Moral Law.[1] His

---

1. Genesis Rabbah, 1 :1.

Will followed the dictates of that Torah—and therefore His work was successful. If the extremists were to base their Will on the Moral Law, much more and much quicker would be their success.

Let us look at the problem of poverty in this land. Is it not ironic that in prosperous America, the richest country on earth, about 20% of its population, white as well as black, are existing in an impoverished state? Here, too, hundreds of books were written and lectures delivered—all offering solutions. Today, the poor are fed up with all these words, and they are determined to have some share in the wealth of the land. And we already see the mighty changes which this show of Will has produced.

Again, consider the problem of War and Peace. On this subject, too, millions of words were spoken and written by great minds, presenting solutions on how to put an end to the evil of war. But all these proposals have been of no efficacy. Today, men and women are beginning to show a *Will* to do away with wars—especially those motivated by economic or colonial imperialism. With the increasing growth of this *Will*, there is hope that Peace will become a realizable goal.

And this truth also applies to the problems facing the Jew and Judaism today.

For 1900 years the Jew prayed, talked and wrote about the restoration of Zion as the Jew's homeland. But, alas, it all remained in the status of *vayomer*, "and he said." Zionism is the movement which transformed this *vayomer* into "and the Jew *Willed*." The present rebirth of Israel is the result of that *Will* to achieve it.

It is significant of the prophetic insight of Theodor Herzl, that, in the famous address which he delivered at the close of the first Zionist Congress, he concluded with that memorable and historic statement: *"Wenn ihr wolt, ist es kein maerchan!"*, "If you but will it, it is no dream!"

And that is the message which Saadya Gaon would bring to us American Jews, who are interested in maintaining and developing our Jewish religious and cultural life in this land. We talk about it, write about it, argue about it—but speech alone will not achieve it. Not *vayomer*, "He said," but *vayomer*, "He *willed*" that His world should come to pass! And so with us Jews. Let us will it—and the chaos that we find in our American-Jewish life will be transformed into a cosmos of healthy, vibrant and beautiful spiritual life.

In all the problems facing us as Americans and as Jews, let us remember Saadya's philosophic insight and the prophetic message of Herzl. Then we shall begin to see the dawn of a new world for mankind and for the Jew, when the Kingdom of Heaven shall reign supreme!

CHILDREN COVERING THE NAKEDNESS
OF THEIR PARENTS*

In the Musaf service of Rosh Hashanah there is a section of the prayers known as *Zichronot*—Memories. We recall certain incidents of the past in order to influence our thoughts and our actions today.

Among these remembrances is one that tells how God was mindful of His love of Noah—"when Thou broughtest forth the waters of the flood to destroy all flesh because of their evil deeds. Thus didst Thou remember him . . ."

We can understand the recalling of the covenant which God entered into with the patriarchs Abraham, Isaac and Jacob, and which applies also to us —their descendants. We can understand, also, the recollection of other great events in the history of our people. But what is the greatness of Noah, that he, too, should be remembered by us of today?

It seems to me that there is one chapter in the life of Noah which is especially relevant to our generation and which it would be wise for us to recall. You remember how Noah, soon after he emerged from the ark—after the flood had ceased—planted a vineyard. "And he drank of the wine and became drunk." The Bible then describes how Noah was naked and wallowed in his drunkenness. And his sons, seeing what happened to their father, "took a

---

* Rosh Hashanah, 1971.

garment . . . walked backward, and covered their
father's nakedness; and their faces were turned
backward, they saw not their father's nakedness."

Something very strange is to be noted in this description. We are told that *"they walked backward"*
—evidently to avoid looking at the father's nakedness. But then the story adds, *"and their faces were
turned backward."* [1] If they walked backward, they
certainly did not need to turn their faces backward
—for then they would indeed behold the nakedness.

Evidently, there is a deeper meaning in the words,
vayelchu achoranis, "and they walked backward."
This phrase is very significant and unfolds the whole
tragedy of the story.

It is perfectly natural for parents to cover the
nakedness of their children. That is the way of the
world. It is a normal going forward in life. But
when children have to cover the nakedness of their
parents, that is *walking backward* in life and in
civilization. That is not progress but regress.

That is the message which the author of this
prayer wanted to impress upon us at this, the holiest,
season of the year.

Were I to analyze the present revolt of youth in
America against their elders—a phenomenon which
has greatly disturbed and shocked many of us—I
would say that it is a revolt against the nakedness
of their parents. They are ashamed of that nakedness. It is an open expression of their revulsion
from the empty lives of their elders, from their low

1. Genesis, 9:20-24.

values, from their worship of the dollar, from their complete dedication to the material things in life. We may not like the methods they use in covering such nakedness, but we must admit that fundamentally, and in large measure, an idealistic strain motivates them and underlies their rebellion. "And they walked backward,"—yea, that is what we are witnessing today, a backward step in the march of life, when children have to cover their parents' nakedness.

There was a time—not so long ago—when parents complained of a lack of idealism on the part of their children. But now things have changed; the youth have become idealistic, and they are covering the nakedness of their elders. They are realizing the shallowness of their parents' lives, their indifference to the great moral and social problems facing the world—wars, racial prejudice, extreme poverty of the masses—all evils wrought by man and which could be eliminated by man; and they are ashamed of that nakedness.

Thoughtful people are beginning to learn the true lessons of this revolt by youth. The cover of Time Magazine, a few months ago, featured a story on this very subject. Its heading was: "How to educate your parents." The editors could have used the Biblical term: "How to cover your parents' nakedness."

The article quotes leading American industrialists, kings in the economic world, who suddenly— through their children—realized their true nakedness. Henry Ford III tells how he was immersed in making money. "I was following the crowd in their views—political, economic and social—until my children had to instill ideals into my mind." The President of Berkeley University in California is quoted as saying, "We are going to see a period in which the young will be our teachers."

We see this clearly among our Jewish young rebels. It is not simply that these youths today may be more educated than their parents. In the old Jewish life, it often happened that the children were more learned than their parents, but the children nevertheless respected their elders because they were not naked; they were garbed in moral wisdom and led idealistic lives.

I remember reading the life story of Palestinian Jewry's first Chief Rabbi—Abraham Isaac Kook, of blessed memory. His father was a learned Jew, but did not match the intellectual and cultural attainments of the gifted son. But when the father entered a room in which the Chief Rabbi sat, no matter what distinguished people were in his company, Rabbi Kook immediately rose from his seat as a mark of respect for his father. He saw his father clothed with the robes of ideals; he saw his keen concern for his people, his deep sympathy with the sufferings of all mankind—a zealous dedication to the spiritual and ethical values of his faith.

Alas, children today do not see such kind of lives in their parents, and they are ashamed of their nakedness.

I recall a scene which I personally witnessed and which left a lasting, sad impression upon me. A number of years ago, a Jew phoned me for an appointment about an urgent, personal matter. As arranged, I met him, his wife and their son. The father, weeping bitterly, told me that the son was planning to marry a non-Jewish girl, who would not be converted, and pleaded that I should dissuade the son from taking this step. Before I had a chance to say a word either to the parents or to the son, the young man rose and, gazing at the father, burst out in anger: "I cannot understand your tears and your weeping. I never saw you show any interest or concern for your Jewish people or religion. I never saw you going to the Synagogue. You never sent me to a Hebrew School. You had me go through a mechanical Bar Mitzvah, because of shame for your neighbors. What suddenly brings you to this outpouring of wrath?" Never, as I did at that hour, have I pitied a parent whose nakedness was so cruelly and pointedly revealed by his own child!

Yes, my friends, perhaps we are witnessing the day when children are becoming teachers of their parents. And this applies not only to younger parents of teen age or college students, but also to older parents who already have older children. The children may not openly revolt, but inwardly, subconsciously, there is a feeling of shame because of the nakedness they see in their parents' lives.

Louis Mumford, in his book, "Technique of Civilization," states: "The discovery of the perfected mirror has made a complete change in the whole progress of civilization." But the mirror, perfected only two centuries ago, allows us to see merely our outward selves—the imperfections of our complexions, our features, our garments, which need to be corrected, to make us look at our best. The mirror does not divulge our inner defects.

Rosh Hashanah and Yom Kippur are spiritual mirrors, which can reveal our inner blemishes. That was the power and the glory of this solemn season in the past. It forced upon the Jew an introspection of his spiritual, moral and intellectual nakedness. He asked himself in the words of our prayer book: *mo anachnu, meh chayenu, mah tzidkosenu,* "What are we? What is our life? What is our righteousness?" And once he realized his failings, he resolved to strive for perfection, and thus to make these "days of awe" what they were intended to be— meaningful and purposeful.

The prayer to which I have alluded, which includes the recollection of Noah, tells us: "And also Noah hast Thou remembered in love,"—and thus, he was saved from destruction. These words apply also to us. Our lives, too, have been saved by God in His love. He gave us, as He gave our parents, the opportunity to escape the barbarism and the cruelties of the old lands, and to come here to enjoy the blessing of freedom which America affords us.

Let us not become drunk in a search for material affluence. Let us not wallow in nakedness. Let us garb ourselves with the robes of righteousness, knowledge and idealism, and thus win the esteem and veneration of our children; so that parents and children may walk together in love and regard for each other, marching forward and not backward, towards that glorious goal—the reign of peace and happiness, of Godliness for all mankind!

WINDOWS IN THE HEAVENS*

In connection with the Biblical account of the world's creation, as told in the first page of the Book of Genesis, an ancient Rabbi adds a beautiful comment that I feel has a particular message for all of us—indeed, for all the world today. He tells us that when God created the world "He installed in the heavens 365 windows which the world was to make use of—182 windows in the east, 182 windows in the west, and one window in the center of the heavens." [1] It is a fanciful tale, of course, depicted in poetic imagery. But that is the way the old Rabbinic masters preferred to express deep truths which had eternal values.

If I were asked what the function is of these solemn days, beginning with Rosh Hashanah and concluding with Yom Kippur, I would say it is to open the window in the Heaven above us—to catch a glimpse of the Divine and to make that vision penetrate and influence our lives. Note that this Rabbinic comment is found in the Talmudic tractate of Rosh Hashanah. Evidently that is the concept which the ancient sages had of the Jewish New Year. Ah, if all of us would heed this interpretation of Rosh Hashanah, how much more meaningful and how much more effective the observance of these solemn days would be!

---

* Rosh Hashanah radio message, Station WOR, Nov. 9, 1945.

1. Jer. Tal., Rosh Hashanah, II : 4; *cf.* Genesis Rabbah, 68 :18.

But our text goes further—it has a universal message for all mankind. The world needs it as well as
the Jews need it. "There are 182 windows in the
east, and 182 windows in the west;" all men, of all
lands, of all faiths, of all races, of all nationalities,
have equal opportunities to open these windows in the
heavens—giving every one the privilege of behold-
ing the Kingdom of the Father of all mankind. It
is this universal note in the Rabbi's comment that
makes it of special significance in our troublesome
age. The vision of heaven is not limited to one na-
tionality, to one color, or to one creed. The windows
to the heavens are equally available to every human
being on earth.

Our text, however, goes still further: "There are
365 windows in the heavens"—a window for every
one of the 365 days in the year! Yea, how important
this phase of the comment is. Every religion—Christian, Moslem, Buddhist, and the countless others—as
well as the Jewish—sponsors special days or seasons
in which we are to cast our eyes heavenward and
gaze through the windows, as it were, for a heavenly
vision to inspire us in our paths of life on earth. We
gather in our respective Houses of Worship, and,
lifting our eyes upward, peer through the window
of heaven for the Divine inspiration that we find so
essential in our earthly life.

But these occasions represent merely the heavenly
glimpse through that one window which God had
fixed in the very center of the heavens. Alas, with the
passing of that special day when the worshippers
leave their sanctuaries, the heavenly windows remain closed, and the heavenly inspiration is gone.

That is the tragedy of the world. Our daily lives have no contact with the windows in the heavens, and the Divine plays no role in our everyday thoughts and deeds. This is the message needed by the peoples of the east and by the peoples of the west —by all mankind.

It is very interesting to note that at the conclusion of the Yom Kippur services, before the Shofar is sounded, the entire congregation rises and proclaims aloud the *Shema*—the affirmation of the belief in the unity of God—and this is followed by another affirmation: "The Lord, He is God," which is repeated aloud seven times—to make clear to the Jew, as he is about to leave the Synagogue, that this declaration is not only for these sacred and solemn days, but also for every one of the seven days of every week that is to appear in the year to come.

What a happier world this would be if all men and women were to habituate themselves to open the windows in the heavens—and to look for their guidance and inspiration, not just when they assemble in their Church or Synagogue, but also in their homes, in their places of business, in office and in market place as well! We would then transport, verily, the heavenly ideals of truth and honor, of justice and righteousness, of love and peace, into our everyday lives, and thus stamp life on earth with the image of heaven.

If we Jews, and all the peoples of the world, would take to heart this lesson, if we would look upward, heavenwards, and daily open the windows to the Source whence cometh our help, then indeed would the coming year be not only a new year but also a happy year for us and for all mankind!

THE STRANGE FIRE ON THE ALTAR OF
THE SANCTUARY—THE STORY OF
THE FIRST GENERATION GAP*

I need hardly tell you how very thankful and grateful I am to our Heavenly Father that He has enabled me once again to stand on this sacred pulpit and to speak once again to this congregation which is so close and so dear to my heart. My physician, before allowing me to preach, demanded a promise that my sermon would be short; and I gave that promise. I hope that I shall be able to keep it.

It is not easy, my friends, for anyone to preach these days. There are so many problems facing us. We are living in a revolutionary age. The whole world is changing before our very eyes, and it is very difficult to find one theme that can serve as a common denominator of all the problems which confront us.

I have nevertheless selected one that I think is important, and I hope, on the other days of the holiday and festival, with God's help, to be able to discuss other significant topics with you. The theme of the sermon this morning is what is popularly known as "The Generation Gap"—the revolt of the young generation against the old.

I take as the text for my sermon the opening verse of the Torah reading of Yom Kippur morning. This verse refers to a tragic incident in ancient Jewish

---

* Kol Nidre, 1968.

life—the sudden and sorrowful death of Nadab and Abihu, sons of Aaron, the high priest.[1] The Bible tells the story of this affair in just two sentences; —but the Rabbis of old wanted to know something more about what had happened. All that the Bible says is that these two young priests brought an *aish zarah*, "a strange fire," on the altar of the sanctuary, and that a fire emanated from God which consumed them.[2] The Rabbis were troubled by this incident. After all, these were not two ordinary young men. They were children from the finest family in ancient Jewish life—the sons of Aaron, the high priest. They were nephews of Moses, the prophet and Law-giver, nephews of Miriam, the prophetess. The Rabbis wanted to know the nature of that *aish zarah*, that "strange fire," that they had brought to the altar of the sanctuary.

Now, a number of traditions about this incident came down from ages past. One rabbi tells us as follows: Those entering the sanctuary marched in a procession,—*Moshe v'Aharon mehalachin techilah*, the leaders were Moses and Aaron—they went first. *V'Nadab v'Avihu mehalchin acharehem.* They were followed immediately by these two young priests; and after them came the Israelites. As they marched in that procession, each of these two young men said to the other, *Matai yamutu shney zekenim halalu*, "When will these two old men die, *v'anu nohagin bisrarah al hatzibur tachtehem*—so that we will take the leadership of the community in their place?"[3] When God heard these words, He became very angry

1. Leviticus, 16:1.
2. Ibid. 10:1,2.
3. Leviticus Rabbah, 20:7; Tanchuma, Achare Mot, 6.

and a fire emanated from Him which consumed
them.

My friends, I think you realize instantly how
vividly this description applies to what we see before
our very eyes today. The young generation is re-
volting against the old; and, while it does not wish
the latter to suffer death, it certainly says to the
old, "You just step aside. You have outlived your
function, your purpose; let us take the leadership
of communal life."

Now, there is really nothing wrong with a desire
by young people to play a leading role in the community. For too long a time we complained of the
estranged younger generation. Its members, we
observed, had little interest in anything except their
own selfish lives. It is therefore good to see them
now wanting to be active in solving the world's
problems. The tragedy, however, is that they want
to do it alone—without the aid of the old.

In speaking of the elderly, we recall from the
Jewish tradition that when a man reaches the age
of sixty, *ben shishim l'ziknah*, he is regarded as an
old man; *ben shivim l'sayvah*, when he is seventy he
has the hoary head, he is an aged man.[4] But these
young people look upon a man of thirty as a *zaken*,
an old man. At thirty, one is already an old fogey
—he has outlived his usefulness, and ought to step
aside.

As I said, it is good that young people should wish
to play a leading part in fashioning life—but for
them to seek to do it alone would be simply a calam-
ity. It is true, youth does have many fine qualities

---

4. Abot, 5:24.

and advantages—youth has strength, vigor, enthusiasm. But it must not forget that the old also have excellent gifts—they have the wisdom and the experience of maturity. To build a new world you need both—you need the qualities of youth and the qualities of the old. Alone, the young can only destroy, not build.

In the pages of the Talmud, there is a beautiful epigram which says, *Binyan yeladim sesirah*—"the building of young people is often just destruction,"[5] not construction. And it is true! When you ask these young folk, especially those of the New Left, "What is your program for the new world?", they readily admit: "We have no program. All we want to do is to destroy the present establishment." That they can do! To destroy—that they can accomplish. But they cannot build a world by themselves.

Now, a second rabbi speaks of another tradition. He tells us: *shenichnesu lamishkan shesuyeh yayin.* "They entered the sanctuary drunk,"[6]—in a state of drunkenness. Mind you, they had to perform the sacred task of keeping the flame on the altar burning; but instead, they entered the sanctuary absolutely drunk, soused with liquor.

I think you see here, too, a picture of what faces us today: the addiction of many of the young—and, I am sorry to say, of many older people who imitate them—to drugs; their extensive use of "pot", heroin, marijuana, LSD. I am not speaking merely of the dangers of these drugs to their bodies and to their minds; for, if you ask these young people, "Why

5. Megillah, 31b; Nedarim, 40a.
6. Lev. R., 20:6; Tanch., Ibid.

this addiction?", they will tell you that the world is filled with so much evil that they do not want to see it any more, they want to escape from it. And these drugs help them to enter "fantasy-land," a sphere of fancy where they see no evil at all.

But, again, my friends, they make a tragic mistake. You cannot rid the world of its evils and you cannot rebuild this world by trying to escape from it into a land of fantasy. If you want to purge the world of evil, you must plunge into the affairs of the world and work, hand in hand with the old, to eradicate the plagues that beset it. Simply escaping into "fantasy-land" will never achieve it. Alas, many of these addicts are not just hippies and yippies, but students coming from fine homes, on the campuses of our leading universities. And unfortunately, too, it must be admitted that a large portion of these smokers of pot are our children—Jewish children. A recent study by a sociologist in California points out that from 30 to 40% of these drug addicts are Jewish young men and Jewish young women. This is a problem that ought to concern us directly.

A third rabbi invokes still another tradition. He tells us that the *aish zarah*, the "strange fire," that they brought to the altar was this: *Shenichnesu mechosre begadim*. "They entered the sanctuary absolutely naked."[7] They cast off not only their sacred vestments, but also their undergarments, and they stood in the sanctuary in their nudity, flaunting their nakedness and flaunting their sexual organs, as if to say, "This is the new wave of life."

My friends, I think that this rabbi could have lived

---

7. Ibid.

in our own day. He gives us an apt portrayal of what our very eyes behold—the all-important role that sex plays in the life of many of our youth.

Now, I don't have to tell you that Judaism, in contrast to classic Christianity, has a very wholesome attitude toward sex. In our Talmud, we have many pages in the tractates dealing with the problems of sex. Our sages recognized that sex is a very important phase of life; but they also recognized that it is not the only important facet.

The tragedy today is that these young people, and, I may add, also many older people who try to be young in this respect, overglorify sex, as if it is the sole significant thing in life; so that, today, with very rare exception, no novel can hope to be on the Best Seller List unless virtually every chapter has a description of a sex orgy. In the motion pictures, no film will be popular unless the beginning, the middle and the end vividly present sexual debauchery. And we have reached the point where, on the stage—in the legitimate theatre—you see nude characters—*mechosre begadim*—utterly without garments, flaunting their nakedness. As one writer aptly noted recently, the current decade will go down not as the decade of the sixties but as the decade of the *sexties*.

Men and women, as I said, we do not minimize the role of sex. What we object to is the deification of sex, its becoming a new religion, its worship as the paramount aspect of life.

And lastly, a fourth rabbi summarizes it all for us. He tells us that in the sanctuary[8] there were

---

8. Ibid. Cf. Etz Yosef to Tanch., ib.

two bins with coal. One was an ordinary bin with ordinary coal—*mibet hakirayim*, to be used to feed the stove, the furnace, when heat was needed in the sanctuary. The other was a bin which was sanctified, and whose coal too was sanctified. It was only the sanctified coal which could be used to feed the flames on the holy altar. But what these two young priests, Nadab and Abihu, did was to take the ordinary coal from the ordinary bin and to try to feed the sacred flame with it. That was the *aish zarah*, the "strange fire"—and they were consumed.

My friends, here in substance is the tragedy that we are witnessing. We have fed the sacred flame on the altar of life with ordinary coals—the vulgarities current in the new day—instead of feeding the flame of life with the sanctified coals—the holy ideals that have come down to us from the ancient past. And if you were to ask me, "What is the function of Rosh Hashanah and Yom Kippur?", I would put it in just these few words: It is an appeal to us, an appeal to all mankind; cease feeding the flame of the altar of life with uncouthness, coarseness and vulgarity, and begin feeding that holy flame with the sacred ideals of true religion—ethical religion— the ideals of the prophets and sages and saints of old. If we shall do that, we shall at least have the hope of being able to build a world rid of evil, and to build a life that will not be a curse but a blessedness to all mankind!

THE MOST SACRED WORD
IN HUMAN LANGUAGE*

There is an interesting comment of the Rabbis on a passage in the Bible that I take as the text for my sermon this solemn eve. The patriarch Jacob had been forced to flee from his parental home because of the threat of his brother Esau to slay him. For twenty years he lived at the home of Laban, whose two daughters he married, and where his children were born. He prospered in his work, and he felt at ease in his new abode. Suddenly, one night, an angel called to him: "Jacob!"—and he immediately responded: *Hineni*, "Here I am!" [1] An ancient Rabbinic translation adds: *b'lashon kudesha oni*, "He answered in a holy language." [2]

This is a very strange comment, difficult to interpret. It is usually understood to mean that Jacob responded in Hebrew, which is known as *lashon kodesh*—and not in Aramaic, the ordinary language of the people in his new abode. In support of this view, an ancient folk statement is offered, that angels understand only Hebrew. [3] But this interpretation is hardly acceptable. Of course Jacob would use Hebrew, his mother tongue, in replying to a Heavenly call. And there really is not much difference between the Hebrew and the Aramaic words for "Here I am."

---

* Kol Nidre, 1969.
1. Genesis, 31:11.
2. Targum Jerusalem, ibid.
3. Cf. Shabbat, 12b.

I believe that there is a deeper meaning to this classic comment. What the author wished to convey is the great truth that he who responds to a Heavenly call to duty, by saying *Hineni*, "Here I am"—ready to perform whatever is asked of him—speaks the *lashon kudesha*, the holiest word in human speech.

That most sacred word was on the lips of the Jew throughout the ages; and the response inherent in that word is one of the secrets accounting for his existence to this very day.

What was the Call that came to Jacob? "Return to thy land!"

It was not easy for Jacob to comply with this demand. After all, he had become accustomed to his new environment. And, especially, the threat of his brother Esau still faced him. Nevertheless, he was true to his word—*Hineni*—ready to perform—and he did return, as the angel had asked.

Today, after 1900 years, this call that Jacob heard comes in emphatic language to all of us Jews—"Return to your land!" How strongly and how persistently our brethren in Israel plead with us—American Jews—to heed that call! And yet how few are those who have responded in that *lashon kudesha*—*Hineni*, "Here I am!"

If, for certain reasons, we cannot respond in the fullest measure, by a physical return—we can, at least, and must speak that sacred word, by offering our financial aid to our Israel brethren in their heroic struggle to preserve the land of Israel from the destructive threats of their enemies. How vital it is for us to speak that word—*Hineni*—if our people's life and our people's land are to be preserved!

This response to a Divine Call is frequently noted in our Bible—uttered by great men in critical hours of our people's life. I limit myself to but a few instances that have special significance for our day.

The next Biblical hero who heard this Call was Moses. Standing before the burning bush, he hears the voice of the Lord: "Moses!" Again, the response is this *lashon kudesha*—"Here I am!" [4] You recall of course what this Call was: to go to Pharaoh and to demand the freedom of those enslaved in the land of Egypt. Here, again, this Divine Call comes to all of us today—and how important it is for us Jews to respond in this holy word—*Hineni!*

I think of the two and a half million Jews in Russia who are in the throes of spiritual bondage, whose religious and cultural life is threatened with extinction by the cruel Communist regime. I realize that we are in a difficult situation—that, unfortunately, we have not the physical power to sway the modern Pharaohs to unloosen these chains of bondage. But, at least, we can protest, and continue to protest, to show our brethren in Russia that we think of them, and feel for them in their plight—to let them know that we have not forgotten them!

And this Call comes to us Jews—and all Americans—to break the chains which still hold so many millions of our Negro brethren, here in America, in economic, educational and social bondage today. And the plight, not only of the blacks, but also of the mil-

---

4. Exodus, 3:4.

lions of impoverished white citizens in this land, who
are literally in economic bondage, should concern us.
How tragic it is that in this richest of all lands, so
many millions—black and white—are virtually
slaves—denied the rights and opportunities of free
human beings. I know the obstacles that face us, the
dangers that confront us, in the extremist reactions
of some of those whom we are to help. But the Divine Call is persistent—to free the enslaved; and our
response must be: *Hineni!*

I come now to another of the immortal figures in
our history—the prophet Isaiah. He, too, heard the
Divine Call: "Whom shall I send, and who will go
for us?" And the prophet immediately responds:
Hineni shelachtani, "Here I am, send me!" [5] Again
this *lashon kudesha*—this most sacred word in human speech. What was this message that came to
Isaiah? To preach the needs of social justice, to de-
nounce prejudice and hatred, to plead for universal
peace—to help turn the swords into ploughshares and
the spears into pruning hooks—to work for the day
when all men would be able to sit under their own
vine and fig-tree, with no one to make them afraid.

Once again, this Divine Call comes to each and
every one of us today. Again we hear the words:
"Whom shall I send?" But, alas, how few of us actually respond in that sacred word, *Hineni!*

If American democracy is to be meaningful—nay,
more, if America is to be preserved—this Divine Call
must be heeded. Fortunately, the conscience of the
American people has lately been stirred to these
needs. We dare no longer be deaf to this Call, but

---

5. Isaiah, 6:8.

must move forward and onward in this quest for universal justice and righteousness.

I have reserved for the conclusion of my message a reference to one who, even before Jacob, spoke this sacred word: the father of our people and the founder of our faith—the patriarch Abraham. He was the first to hear this Divine Call. "Abraham, Abraham!" And instantly his response came, in that most sacred of all words—*Hineni!*[6] You recall, of course, what the Call was. It is the theme of one of the Torah readings on the New Year: A test of Abraham's faith in his God—a most difficult test. He was asked to take his only and beloved son and to offer him as a sacrifice on the altar of the Lord. And Abraham, true to his response, was ready to perform this demand and to prove how sincere his faith was.

We Jews in America hear this Divine Call today. We call ourselves Jews, we speak of our religion, of our spiritual and cultural ideals. We say we want Judaism to survive in this blessed land. Are these words just utterances of our lips, or do we sincerely believe in them? Are we willing to make sacrifices to prove the sincerity of our words—and also to do all in our power to assure the meaningful survival of Judaism in this land?

Thank God we are not asked to sacrifice any lives to meet this test. We are asked to give only thought, work, resources, and, above all, concern, for the future of our spiritual life.

This very Center, in which we are now assembled, and which has made such glorious contributions to-

---

6. Genesis, 22:1.

wards Jewish survival in America, was the result of the response of a small group of Jews. Just fifty years ago, they heard the Divine Call which had come to Abraham, and they spoke that holy word, *Hineni*, ready to prove the sincerity of their desire that Judaism should continue to live.

Today, as we usher in the Jubilee year of our Center's existence, the Call comes once again to each and every one of us—and the destiny of our religion depends in large measure on whether or not we will respond in that sacred word.

From every side, the old spiritual values of religion are being challenged. A vulgar, materialistic nihilism is offered as a substitute for the ancient prophetic ideals. If ever in all the years past, spiritual lighthouses, such as our Center, have been needed, they are so much the more needed today!

Another sage, also commenting on this word, *Hineni*, tells that it is *lashon neviim*—the language of the Prophets[7]. True, we are not prophets, but all of us are the *b'nai neviim*—descendants of the Prophets—and in that capacity, too, it is incumbent upon us to learn to speak that sacred word.

On this day, as we begin the commemoration of our Jubilee year, may our ears be attuned to these ancient Divine Calls, which so clearly still reverberate, and may each of us respond in that sacred and prophetic word—*Hineni*—Here I am, ready to fulfill my duty as a Jew and as an American. Thus we will help to bring nearer the day when the chains of all forms of bondage will be shattered; and then true liberty of body and soul will reign in our lives and in the lives of all men!

---

7. Torah Shelemah, Genesis, 31 :11, Note 22.

DREAMING OF THE ETHROG*

There is a strange but very interesting statement of the Rabbis that I wish to interpret for you on this festival of Sukkot, because of its great relevance for our day. "He who sees an *Ethrog* in a dream is regarded as beautiful before his Maker!" [1] How out of date and outmoded these words seem to sound! Let us look a little deeper into this statement, and we shall find, I believe, a vital message which all the world needs.

Dreams troubled all ancient peoples. And, even today, psychologists and psychiatrists have written much about the phenomenon of dreams. Sigmund Freud, the father of modern psychoanalysis, has contributed important studies on this theme. The Jews of old were concerned about this subject, and the Bible has many references to the role that dreams have played in the lives of our ancient heroes. We recall the dream of Jacob—of the ladder reaching unto the heavens; the dreams of Joseph—which played such an important part in the events of his life; and the dreams of Pharaoh—which changed the life of Joseph as well as the life of our ancestors. Many more references to dreams are scattered in the Bible —a circumstance showing how significantly they were considered by the people.

The Rabbis in the Talmud were not formal psychologists or psychiatrists; and yet they possessed—

---

* Sukkot, 1972.
1. Berachot, 57a.

to a remarkable degree—intuitive insights into human nature, which reveal a profound understanding of psychological truths.

What are dreams? And why should one dream of a specific subject? In the same Talmudic study which begins the discussion on dreams, one Rabbi tells us: "all dreams *holchin achar hapeh*, follow the utterances of the mouth."[2] When a person talks a great deal about a certain subject, when his mind is steadily concentrated on that theme, the probability is, according to this sage, that he will dream of it in his sleep. This is a conclusion which modern psychologists, too, accept. The philosopher, Montaigne, of the sixteenth century, uttered a similar observation: "I believe it to be true that dreams are the true interpreters of our inclinations."[3]

Now, I think, we can begin to understand the wisdom inherent in the Rabbinic statement of the great importance of one's dreaming about the *Ethrog*, and of how such dreamer is regarded by his Maker.

The Rabbis saw similarities between each of the four Sukkot plants and certain parts of the human body. The Ethrog, they tell us, *domeh l'lev*, "resembles the human heart." [4] If you examine the shape of this beautiful fruit, you will immediately see how clear the resemblance is.

The tragedy of the world today is that the subject of the human heart is no longer on our lips. We no longer talk about it, nor do our minds concentrate upon it. We therefore no longer dream of the Ethrog.

2. Ibid., 55 b.
3. Essays, Book III, ch. 13.
4. Leviticus Rabbah, 30:14.

In discussing which Ethrog is valid for use in the recital of the blessings, the Rabbis emphasize that *lim'eute ethrog yavesh*, "a dried, shrivelled citron may not be used."[5] Here, again, is revealed the world's tragedy. Our hearts are like the *ethrog yavesh*—dried and shrivelled. They have lost all feeling, all sensitivity—and therefore lack the power to improve the status of mankind. We no longer dream of the ethrog—the human heart—and that is a primary reason for the wars, the racial hatred, the religious prejudices and the poverty, which afflict the world today.

The human mind has grown and developed. Man has conquered space. He can walk on the moon. But the human heart is still in the jungle. The prophet's words addressed to King Nebuchadnezzar of Babylon may be applied to modern man: "And thou saidst in thy heart: 'I will ascend unto heaven; above the stars of God will I exalt my throne; ... I will ascend above the heights of the clouds; I will be like the Most High!' Yet thou shalt be brought down to the nether-world, to the uttermost parts of the pit."[6]

While the mind has advanced, the human heart has remained the heart of the savage. The Rabbis have a phrase summarizing it all in a few words: *Hakadosh baruch Hu liba ba'i*, "The Holy One Blessed be He wants the human heart!"[7]

The world is seeking an answer to all its problems. The Rabbis offer the answer: Begin to concentrate on the heart in all our waking hours—and we

5. Sukkah, *29* b.
6. Isaiah, 14:13-15.
7. Sanhedrin, 106 b.

shall then dream of the *pri etz hadar*, the beautiful fruit—the *Ethrog*. If we will do so, we shall, in the words of the ancient Rabbis, be regarded as beautiful before our Maker!

THE TWO GATES
OF KING SOLOMON'S TEMPLE*

The festival of Sukkot and the concluding day of Shemini Atzeret, in addition to having other meanings, commemorate the completion and dedication of the first Temple built in Jerusalem by King Solomon. On the second day and the last days of the festival, we read for the Haphtorah lessons the portions in the Bible narrating the beginning and the conclusion of the dedication exercises. [1]

The Bible presents a detailed description of the magnificent structure which was to serve the children of Israel as their most sacred shrine—the size, the kind of wood and ornamentation, the various special metals, even the unique type of windows.[2]

The Rabbis give an additional touch to the Biblical portrayal: "When Solomon built the Holy Temple he made *shne sha'arim*, two gates for the people's entrance—one for bridegrooms, and one for mourners and those depressed. And when the High Priest arrived every morning to offer his sacrifices, he would look and observe—if the *sha'ar hasimchah pasuach*, if the gate of joy was open, he would pronounce praise and thankfulness to the Lord. But when the *sha'ar ha-avelim pasuach*, the gate of mourners was open and the gate of joy closed, he would prostrate himself in prayer to seek mercy in behalf of his people." [3]

---

* Shemini Atzeret, 1966.
1. I Kings, Chap. 8.
2. Ibid, Ch. 6.
3. Pirke d' R. Eliezer, 17.

[45]

What a beautiful and meaningful thought the Rabbis convey and what a vital message it offers us today! It was the glory of Jewish life throughout the ages that its sanctuaries always had these *shne sha'arim*, these two gates, and that both gates were ever open.

The Jew never forgot his beloved ones who were gone, and he came to the synagogue on various occasions to recall their lives and their memories and, through his prayers, to derive inspiration for the tasks of life facing him. And those who were depressed also utilized this gate of sadness to enter the sanctuary and to find strength and courage to help raise their spirits.

But the Jew never permitted only the gate of mourners to remain open, and the *sha'ar hasimcha sagur*, the gate of joy closed. That gate too was wide open, and the Jew utilized it throughout his life, not only on joyous events but also on all other days, especially the Sabbaths and Festivals, to offer thanks for the happy and blessed gifts of life and health which our Divine Father had bestowed upon him and his dear ones.

The great tragedy in our religious life at present is that this description of our sanctuaries of the past has ceased having effect. The *sha'ar hasimcha* no longer functions. It is, alas, only the *sha'ar ha-avelim* which is open! Contrast the attendance in all synagogues—orthodox, conservative, reform and reconstructionist—on the first days of Sukkot and this day when the *Yizkor*, the Memorial services, are held, and you see how the American Jew fails to exemplify the wisdom of Solomon. We have reached a stage of religious life where congregations advertise in the press that *Yizkor* will be held every half hour —from 9:30 A.M. to 12:30 P.M.—without even mentioning that a regular festival prayer service will be conducted or a sermon delivered—as if only the use of the gate of mourners was essential!

I do not for a moment mean to belittle the importance of the *Yizkor*. I am happy when I see children, whether young or old, wanting to remember parents, who are no longer in the land of the living. It is an important precept of religion—but not the only one. *Vochai bohem*, thou shalt live by them; the precepts of our faith are to regulate or guide our daily lives. And it is through the Synagogue, and the frequent use of it, that our lives become enriched, meaningful and purposeful.

Frequent polls are taken of Church and Synagogue attendance, and the results are generally publicized in the press. I am always pained at reading the data. A recent poll showed Catholics in the lead with a 60% attendance; Protestants came next with a rating of 48-50%; and Jews followed with 35%. Attendance was considered not on a regular weekly basis but on at least three Saturdays or Sundays in the month. I do not know how you react to such statistics, but, as for myself, I suffer a sense of shame.

I am reminded of a striking passage in the *Kuzari*, by the great Hebrew philosopher and poet, R. Jehudah Halevi. In arguing in behalf of Judaism before the King of the Khazars, who was seeking the most acceptable religion, the Chaver, or Jewish scholar, spoke, among other things, of the exalted role which

Palestine played in Judaism. As he was becoming ecstatic in praise of the land, the King interrupted him, saying: "If Palestine means so much to you, how is it that you are here and not in Palestine?" *Hibashtani, melech Khazar*—"You have put me to shame, King of Khazar!" He really had no answer.

That is how I feel whenever I read the results of these polls. We Jews gave the concept of the holy Sanctuary to the world; we Jews gave the notion of the Sabbath to all the nations. Nevertheless, we are prone to forsake the Synagogue except in times of sorrow.

Yes, when the High Priest, on entering the Temple, saw the gate of the mourners open and the gate of joy closed, he prostrated himself in prayer to seek mercy for his people. The spiritual leaders of American Jewry, these days, looking at the two gates of our synagogues and temples must too, alas, offer such prayer of mercy for our people.

May we now resolve once again to keep the *sha'ar hasimchah*, the gate of joy, wide open! Let us enter this gate as well as the gate of mourners, and we shall soon learn to say with the Psalmist: "I rejoiced when they said to me 'Let us go to the House of the Lord' ". [4]

---

4. Psalms, 122:1.

THE BOWL OF OIL IN THE MENORAH*

The Rabbis have assigned a very interesting section of the Bible for the Haftorah, the Scriptural reading in the synagogue, on the Sabbath of the festival of Hanukkah.[1] We are to read of the vision of the Prophet Zechariah, in which he beheld "a candlestick all of gold, with a *gulah*—a bowl—upon the top of it, and its seven lamps thereon; there are seven pipes, yea, seven, to the lamps on the top of it."[2]

We can readily understand how the Rabbis connected this vision with the Hanukkah festival; for this holiday marks the dramatic rekindling of the *Menorah*, the sacred candelabrum, recalling the rededication of the Holy Temple by the Maccabees after their great victory over the Graeco-Syrians, and the miracle of the cruse of oil which, although sufficient for only one day's kindling, burned for eight days.[3]

When the prophet Zechariah had this vision of the candlestick with a *gulah*, he wanted to know its significance and asked the angel: "What are these, my Lord?" He was told: "This is the word of the Lord, Not by might, nor by power, but by My spirit, saith the Lord of hosts." [4]

---

* Sabbath Hanukkah, 1959.
1. Zechariah, 2:14-4:7.
2. Ibid., 4:2.
3. Shabbat, 21 b.
4. Zechariah, 4:6.

It is striking to note that on the very festival when we recall the superb military victory of the Maccabees we proclaim the message of God, "Not by might, nor by power, but by My spirit," as if to emphasize that victories on battlefields offer no definitive answer to a people's problems. Though wars may be necessary in order to defend oneself, real assurance of salvation is gained only by upholding the lamp of the spirit and the law of God.

But there is another message of this prophet particularly applicable to American Jews today. Zechariah lived in an age similar, in many ways, to our own. He had been born in Babylon not long after the destruction of the Temple and the dispersion of the Jews to that country. He had witnessed the issuance of the proclamation of King Cyrus, the conqueror of Babylon, permitting the Jews to return to Jerusalem and to rebuild the Temple. Only a small fraction of the exiles, forty-two thousand, returned; the rest decided to remain in Babylon. Only fifty years had elapsed since the dispersion, but the majority of the Jews had already become acclimatized to the different surroundings. They began to prosper there, and they chose to continue in this new land.

Later, the prophet himself returned to Jerusalem. He saw the struggle of the little band of the men and women who returned to put life into the devastated soil, and he witnessed their hardships in warding off the obstacles and hindrances of the Samaritans who sought to prevent their rebuilding the Temple. Thus he knew the life of the Jews in both lands, in Babylon and in Judea.

It was then that the vision of the Menorah came to him. He saw the candelabrum, with the bowl for oil on top, and seven pipes emerging from the bowl, through which the oil passed into the seven lamps that fed the light. The Rabbis noticed that the Hebrew word employed here for bowl—*gulah*—was unusual and infrequently used. In the description of the first Menorah placed in the tabernacle of the wilderness, the Torah uses *g'via*[5], the regular Hebrew word for cup or bowl. Thus the Rabbis attached special significance to the different term adopted by Zechariah. One Rabbi said that it was to remind us of a similarly sounding word, *geulah*, redemption; a second Rabbi said that it was to remind us of another similarly sounding word, *golah*, dispersion or diaspora.[6]

Here, then, is the message which Zechariah wanted to bring to his fellow Jews, particularly to those in Babylon. They represented the *gulah* of the Menorah, the bowl of substance that was to nourish the light of Jewish life. It was to be their privilege and their obligation to provide the resources that would illuminate and foster Jewish life in the land of the *geulah*, the land that was being redeemed. They dared not leave that sacred task to be done alone by the small band of heroic men and women who had returned to Judea. They had to be partners in the enterprise. And Babylonian Jewry accepted the prophet's challenge and indeed served as the *gulah*, the bowl of sustenance for the Menorah which was being fashioned in the land of the *geulah*, Judea. Though they remained in Babylon, their hearts overflowed with love for their brethren who

---

5. Exodus, 25:31 f.
6. Leviticus Rabbah, 32:7.

had returned to the Holy Land and who were making great sacrifices to rekindle the Menorah of Jewish ideals in their historic home.

But Zechariah reminded his fellow Jews in Babylon of a further duty, to feed the lights of the Menorah so as to sustain and to nourish their own Jewish spiritual and cultural life in the *golah*, the land and the community of the diaspora, Babylon. They could not long survive in that new environment without kindling the lights of the Menorah in their *golah*. And Babylonian Jewry also took to heart this message of the prophet. It was primarily in Babylon that the institution of the Synagogue was fashioned. It developed there not only as a House of Prayer but also as a House of Study and a House of Assembly for old and young. Schools were established in Babylon which were the seeds for the great academies and seats of learning blossoming there centuries later. Babylonian Jewry served as the *gulah*— the bowl of oil—which fed the lights of the Menorah both in the land of the *geulah*, reborn Judea, and in the *golah*, the land of Babylon—and thereby saved Jewish life in both communities.

We, Jews in America, are reliving history, and the prophet's message has the same significance for us today. Thank God that we have lived to see the birth of Israel's third commonwealth. While more than a million Jews from many parts of the world have returned, we must acknowledge that only a handful of American Jews are among them. We hope, of course, that many more will return to link their lives with those of their brethren in the pioneering task of rebuilding the old-new land. We are realists, however, and recognize that the rank and file of American Jews are determined to make America their home.

The prophet's message must nevertheless be taken to heart. American Jewry is privileged and blessed to play the role of the *gulah*, the bowl, richly laden with the substance needed to kindle a living Menorah in the land of the *geulah*, redeemed Israel. We have to keep feeding the lights already rekindled there so that they may glow with ever greater strength and beauty. American Jewry, thank God, is helping in that task. I am confident that most American Jews are conscious of this sacred obligation and will participate in the much greater efforts that can and should be exerted for the land of Israel.

And, like the Babylonian Jews, we, too, must feed the lights of the Menorah in the land of the *golah*—in our case, America! American Jewry, the largest Jewish community in the world, cannot hope to perpetuate Jewish life here by acquiring material success alone. "Not by might nor by power"—that is the significant warning of the prophet to us as well. We can live as Jews only if we kindle in our lives and in the lives of our children the spirit of our living God. It is through our synagogues, our Hebrew and religious schools, our institutions of Hebrew culture, our yeshivot, our seminaries and our colleges of Jewish learning, that the lights of our Menorah can be made to burn brightly so as to illumine Jewish life in America.

Fortunately, American Jewry has it within its power to accomplish this two-fold task. The Rabbis said of Joseph in Egypt: *sipek b'yado laasot*, "it was within his power to do things"; *l'fi shehashaah mesurah lo*, "for the hour was opportune for him."[7] Or, as another sage put it beautifully: *shehashaah mesacheket lo*, "for the hour smiled for him."[8] So, too, it may be said of American Jewry: "If we but will it, we have the power to achieve it, the hour is smiling for us." Paraphrasing Joseph, we can fortunately say: "For God sent us in front of you to be a preserver of life."

Let us be grateful to God that we are privileged to play the role of the *gulah* for the *geulah* and for the *golah*, and so be imbued with the will and determination to do all within our power to help fashion a thriving, beautiful, Jewish life in Israel and in America!

---

7. Genesis Rabbah, 96:5.
8. Matnot Kehunah, ibid.

THE PLAGUE OF DARKNESS IN EGYPT*

We are all familiar with the account of the ten plagues which God had inflicted upon the Egyptians in order to force the unwilling Pharaoh to free his Israelite slaves.

The Bible describes these plagues in detail;[1] and we recite a summary of them in the Passover Haggadah, as we sit at the Seder table on the eve of the festival.

One of the severest of these afflictions was the plague before the last—that of darkness. The Bible describes it in keen fashion: "It was a thick darkness," "a darkness which may be felt." "They saw not one another, neither rose any from his place." [2]

This is the rendition given in the English translation originally published by the Jewish Publication Society many years ago. It is also the version, with slight variations, appearing in practically every other edition of the English Bible.

In the new Torah translation recently published under the aegis of a group of well-known Bible scholars, as well as by the Jewish Publication Society, the text is rendered: "People could not see one another and no one could get up from where he was."

But all these translations—new and old—are really paraphrases, not translations. None of them

---

* Passover, 1969.
1. Exodus, ch. 7-11.
2. Ibid., 10:22, 23.

[55]

goes to the heart of what the Hebrew text seemingly tells us: *Lo kamu ish mitachtav*—"No one could get up from where he was." But the Hebrew text does not say this at all!

No matter how dark a place may be, nor how thick the darkness, one can certainly stand up from where he is sitting and sit down again when he wishes. Fearful that he might stumble if he tried to walk or that he might not be able to return to his original place, he may not venture to leave his seat. But surely one can rise or get up from where he is.

The literal translation of these words, however, does give us the true—and an altogether different— meaning: *Lo kamu* "They did not rise, *ish mitachtav*, any from his *lower self!*" That is the real meaning of this verse. The description of the darkness which God brought upon the Egyptians portrays not only the physical aspect of the plague itself but also the spiritual darkness that reigned in Egypt and that was the cause of all the other plagues.

The tragedy described in the Hebrew text was the extreme selfishness of the Egyptians—no one rising *mitachtav*, from his lower self, from his lowest and basest instincts!

And that kind of civilization was brought about by the truth revealed in the first part of the text— *lo ra-oo ish es achiv*, "they did not see each his brother." No one perceived the brother in his fellow man!

That, alas, is the darkness now plaguing mankind in so many parts of the world! That is the reason for the rivers of blood, for the pestilence, for the thick darkness, infesting the world today.

Only when man will learn to see his brother in his fellow-man, when man will learn to rise *mitach-tav*, from his lower self, can we hope that the plagues which torment him will disappear from the face of the earth!

THE FOUR SONS OF THE HAGGADAH*

One of the fascinating sections of the Haggadah, which we recite at the Seder table, is that describing the four different types of children—the wise, the wicked, the simple, and the one who does not know enough to ask.

This description is based on four separate verses in the Bible,[1] in three of which "thy son" is mentioned and in one where reference is made to "thy children," and where the parent is enjoined to tell them the story of the Exodus.

A play upon these Biblical verses is inserted in the Haggadah for the special purpose of interesting the children and of keeping even the youngest awake at the Seder table. I remember that, when I was a child, this characterization served the children of our family as a sort of game, in which each would tease the others, as, who was the *chacham* or the *tam* or the *she'eno yode'a lishol;* no one of course would dare to call another the *rasha.*

I should like to go into a deeper analysis of these four types of children presented by the author of the Haggadah, because I feel that it offers a vital message for parents—even more than for children.

If we pause at the very first word of the Hebrew passage—*k'neged*—we note something strange. The

---

* Passover, 1968.
1. Deut., 6:20; Exodus, 12:26; 13:8; 13:14.

author evidently wanted to state that "The Torah speaks *k'neged arbaah banim,* of, or about, four sons or children" (The word *banim* means both sons and children). There are, however, a number of Hebrew words which could have been used instead of *k'neged.* This word really implies something *neged, against,* all of the four types—including the *chacham,* the "wise one". It seems the author was opposing something not only in the other three, which we can all understand, but also in the make-up of the so-called "wise son". With all his supposed wisdom, there is an essential quality which this *chacham* lacks.

Some of you, versed in the Yiddish language, will recall the folk saying, *"a chacham fun ma nishtana",* or *"a chacham fun die Haggadah".* When one wants to ridicule a person who thinks he uttered a word of wisdom, whereas the listener thinks it's foolish, he will speak of him as *"the chacham"* described in this very section of the Haggadah.

What is wrong with this *chacham?* He asks a very intricate and worth-while question, one going deep into the philosophy of Jewish law and practice: "What are the *edos, v'hachukim, v'hamishpatim,* the testimonies, the statutes and the judgments which the Lord our God commanded you"? It is a very apt question, indeed—but one which cannot be answered while the so-called wise one stands on one foot. The answer which the father is to give him according to our author, is very significant: "Tell him *k'hilchos hapesach"*—usually translated as "the laws of Passover." But the Hebrew expression does not say that at all! If that were the real meaning of this statement, the words would be: *hilchot hapesach* "the laws of Passover." The Hebrew rendering, however, is *k'hilchos*, "*like* the laws of Passover"—an altogether different meaning.

At the outset, as we sit down for the Passover ceremony, we are given a procedure—a *Seder*—a systematized order for observance. And the *chacham* is advised by the father: "Your question is good, but to understand the reply you have to follow *k'hilchos*, like the procedure of this Seder: *Kadesh* —you must sanctify or dedicate yourself to Jewish study; your questions can't be answered in a moment or even in an hour. *Urchatz*, you must cleanse yourself of your Jewish ignorance, you must immerse yourself in Jewish learning. *Magid*—study! *Shulchan aruch* 'the table is prepared', the vast literature is all ready for you; all you have to do is to make use of it". If this *chacham* would follow *k'hilchos hapesach*—like this procedure—he could hope to recite the *Hallel*, the hymns of praise, for having become the real *chacham*, the truly wise son, who will have a genuine appreciation of his people's spiritual heritage.

This portrayal illustrates the trouble with so many of the Jewish intellectuals of our day. They ask for instant answers to their questions and criticism concerning Judaism, not realizing that a cultural and spiritual tradition of thousands of years requires diligent study and extensive learning for it to be understood and appreciated.

We come now to the description of the second type —the *rasha*, the wicked one. Note that in his case he does not ask at all. The reference to him in the Bible does not say: "And when your son *yishalcha,* will ask you"—as it says in the case of the *chacham* or of the *tam*—but it says *ki yomru alechem*, "when your sons will *say* to you." He asks no questions, he tells you "the thing"—what he thinks of the whole matter. He does not even wait for an answer. Incidentally, some readers may recall that, in pictorial representations in editions of the Haggadah published many years ago, the *rasha* was depicted as standing on one foot—as if he were running. That is a very good portrayal; he tells you "the thing" as he sees it—he waits for no reply.

The response of the parent, given by the author of the Haggadah—*hakhe es shinav*, "set his teeth on edge," or, more literally, "strike or knock out his teeth"—an advice, by the way, not suggested in the Biblical text—will not do today. The *rasha*, who no longer respects his parents, will strike back—physically, he is the stronger one. Arguments with him are not possible, and would be to no avail—*shehotzi es atzmo min haklal*, "he has removed himself from the Jewish fold." It is too late to bring him back now. He is the fallen leaf from the tree of Jewish life. The description of him in the Haggadah can serve only as a warning to other parents to do all that is possible, while the child is young, to prevent him from becoming a *rasha*.

Something else is to be noted, as we think of the *rasha*. Of the four children, he is the only one of whom the Bible speaks in the plural—*binchem*, "your sons." Each of the others is referred to in the singular—*bincha*, or "your son." Unfortunately, this type of child is increasing in our midst, and is often the result of parental neglect in the years gone by.

The third child—the *tam*, the "simple one" does offer us some hope. *Ma zos*, "what is all this?" he asks, as he views the Seder procedure. He may not be overbright, as is the *chacham*. But at least he wants to know. He realizes that he missed the learning which he should have received. He sees his cultural nakedness. The problem here is not with the *tam*, "the simple one," but with his parents. It is a challenge to them, which the author of the Haggadah hopes the parents will accept, for this child can yet be saved to Jewish life.

The concluding type—the *she'eno yode'a lishol*, the one who does not know even to ask,—indeed is the worst of all! No wonder that the author places him last. One might think that the wicked one is the worst and should come last in the description. But no; the author is correct in his enumeration. With the *rasha*, we know where he stands—he has already excluded himself from the body of the Jewish community. But this fourth type presents more serious problems. He is the indifferent one. Not only does he not know what to ask; he is not even interested in knowing. What a tragedy he represents in our communal life!

There is, however, one redeeming feature about him. He, at least, would listen if the parent spoke to him. He does not ask, but he would not turn a deaf ear to someone who addressed him and tried to awaken his interest. And the wise author of the Haggadah offers the parent good advice. *Att p'sach lo* "You begin for him!" It is for the parent to begin the process of communication with this child, to start to tell him what he ought to know.

And the author pertinently points out that the challenge is to both parents—to father and mother alike, and not to one parent alone.

Note the wording in the text *Att p'sach lo.* In Hebrew the subject (noun or pronoun) must always conform to the gender of the verb, and vice versa. Here, however, the pronoun *att* is feminine while the verb *p'sach* is masculine, which is most unusual. The wording should have been either both in the masculine or both in the feminine. I think, though, that the author used the mixed forms intentionally, to teach us that the challenge must be met by the mother *and* the father, so that the indifferent child may hopefully become interested enough to ask and to want to know.

And I have a feeling that the author gives this same advice at the conclusion of the entire chapter, to make us realize that his formula applies not merely to the indifferent child but to all four. If a solution is at all possible to make all the types of children real *chachamim*, wise and learned, and conscious of their obligation to their faith and to their people, the only hope lies in the fulfillment of these few words: *Att p'sach lo!* You, the parents, "open up", make the beginning; initiate the dialogue! You, of course, must first know what to say and how to answer the children. If the parents will be culturally and spiritually equipped "to open up," to begin the process of communication, then, and only then, can we hope that the words of the Prophet will be fulfilled, "And all Thy children shall be learned of the Lord";[2] to which the Rabbis signifi-

---

2. Isaiah, 54:13.

cantly add, "Read, not *banayich*, your children, but *bonoyich*, your builders",[3] for they will then become true builders of the Jewish life and the Jewish future!

---

3. Berachot, end.

THE JEW'S BANNER OF SALVATION*

On this, the seventh day of the Passover festival, we read for our Torah lesson the majestic song of triumph which Moses and the children of Israel sang after safely crossing the Red Sea. The waters had miraculously divided, enabling the Israelites to walk on dry paths. After they had landed on the other shore, the waters rejoined, drowning the pursuing Egyptians.

It was then that Moses and the other Israelites burst forth into words of song, at the very beginning of which they cried out: *azi v'zimrat yah*, "The Lord is my strength and my song," *vayehi li liyeshuah*, "and He is become my salvation."[1]

This is the usual translation given in the original English version, published by the Jewish Publication Society, and in many other English translations of the Bible.

A new translation, recently made by the Jewish Publication Society, gives a different rendition of this verse: "The Lord is my strength and *my might* and He is become my salvation." Note that the distinguished Bible scholars who made the new translation, changed the word *v'zimrat* from "*my song*" to "*my might*"—a very daring change.

The root word *zimra*, it is true, is the usual Hebrew word for song; but it also has the added

---

* Seventh day of Passover, 1965.
1. Exodus, 15:2.

meaning of might or power. Indeed, the greatest of our Bible commentators, Rashi, already notes—under this very verse—that *Zimrat* in this passage does not refer to song, and he suggests another translation.

The new rending, "My strength and my might," reveals a very interesting insight into this beautiful verse, which appears twice in the Bible—here, in the song of the Israelites, and later in the Psalms,[2] where the author again praises God for being his help when the nations conspired to destroy him and his people.

There is justification for the new translation of *v'zimrat*, as "might" or "power".[3] It appears that in the cognate poetry of the other ancient, Semitic peoples, it was customary to use parallelisms to express the same thought. The present translation, therefore, has more emphatic meaning than the usual rendering. The word *azi*, "my strength," is paralleled by the word *v'zimrat*, "my might."

The question which I wish to pose goes deeper into the true meaning of this verse—especially in the new rendering of the word *v'zimrat*. It should be, according to all rules of grammar, *v'zimrati*, "and my might." The word *v'zimrat* is in the construct state, and cannot refer to the might of the speaker or singer.

I put this question one summer to a noted Biblical student, a member of the Melton Group, whom I had met at Camp Ramah. Referring to ancient

2. Psalms, 118:14.
3. See "Notes on the New Torah Translation" edited by Prof. Harry Orlinsky, P. 170.

Semitic poetry, he gave a scientific explanation, namely, that often the last syllable in the parallel word in such verses is omitted.

Whatever the scientific explanation may be, I think we have the right to translate this verse in its literal sense. This offers us, in the spirit of the Midrash, an altogether new insight into the genius of the Jew—how man is to meet the challenges of life, and also a new revelation of the Jewish belief in God.

I venture to offer the following translation, which I believe was the intent of the author: *azi* "My strength", *v'zimrat yah*, "*and the might of God, vayehi li liyeshuah*—that has been my salvation."

Not reliance on my power alone, nor reliance on God's might alone, was to be the salvation of the Jew —but a reliance on the powers of both. The Jew could never and would never utter the words "my strength alone has achieved it." On the other hand, his Jewish instinct taught him not to rely only on God. There was to be a spiritual partnership between the two: God was to be the source of the Jew's inspiration; faith in Him and in His help and support was to be the directive spirit. But the Jew was to be the active instrument to achieve what had to be done.

The very experience which the Israelites underwent in the crossing of the Red Sea is beautifully revealed in the words of our text. God was the directing force when He said to Moses: "Speak to the children of Israel that they go forward!" But the waters did not divide nor the miracle occur until, as the Rabbis tell, the Israelites had first plunged into the waters and the waters had reached *ad chotman*

their nostrils. Only then—after the evidence of the
Jew's sacrificial action—did the waters divide and
were the Israelites able to walk on dry paths.[4] No
wonder that the Jew at the very opening of his song
of triumph and gratitude, sang out: "My strength
and the might of God, that was my salvation!"

And the Bible concludes the verse with the same
refrain: *Zeh Eli v'anvehu*, "This is my God, and I
will glorify Him." The Rabbis of old saw deeper
into these words than what our present translations
offer: "This is my God, *v'anvehu—ani v'hu*, I and
He![5]

Israel Abrahams, in his "Festival Studies," [6] gives
a delightful picture of the procession around the
altar with the *lulav* and *ethrog*, and offers the same
free translation of the Mechilta to the refrain repeated by the Jew, *ani v'ho hoshe'a na*, "I and He,
save now!"

That was the banner of the Jew throughout the
ages. And that was his concept of the role of God
in his life. Not his own strength alone was his salvation, nor was his salvation in God's mighty
power alone. It is only this spiritual partnership—
my strength, *v'zimrat yah*, and the inspiration and
directive power of God—that has been and ever will
be the salvation of the Jew!

---

4. Exodus Rabbah, 21 :9.
5. Mechilta to this verse; also Shabbat, 133.b; Rashi, ibid.
6. P. 12.

ASLEEP OR AWAKE*

There is an old custom, still observed by many of the devout, for Jews to be awake the entire night of the festival of Shavuot. Throughout the night they recite certain parts of the Scriptures and special prayers designed for the occasion. The custom is termed *Tikun lel Shavuot*, "the special program for the night of *Shavuot*."

The sages attribute the origin of this custom to the Biblical scene at Mount Sinai, at the time of God's revelation of the Torah. "God said to Moses . . . And they shall be prepared for the third day, for on the third day the Lord will descend on the mountain of Sinai in the sight of all the people." [1] A few verses later Moses repeats these words to the people. [2] One would imagine that, having heard what would take place on the promised day, and in anticipation of the unusual forthcoming event, the people would not be able to sleep on that fateful night. But what happened? "And on the morning of the third day," the Bible recounts—to which an ancient Rabbi adds—"The Israelites slept soundly during that night, and the Holy One blessed be He appeared on the mountain and lo—no one was there! They were all fast asleep. And He brought thunder and lightning, and caused the Shofar to be sounded

---

* Shavuot, 1969.
1. Exodus, 19:11.
2. Ibid., 19:15.

very strongly, but they still slept. And Moses had to awaken them, and he actually led them almost forcibly to the mountain before God. Said R. Yitzchak, this is the rebuke of God, referred to by the prophet: Why did I come and no one was there; I called and no one answered?" [3]

To this awesome description of what happened at Sinai, later Rabbis add this meaningful explanation: "To atone for this slumber on the night before the great event at Sinai it was decreed that the Jews should be awake throughout the night of the festival for ages to come!"[4]

What a remarkable and significant interpretation this is! And how relevant it is for our day! If people are asleep when they should have been awake, they are destined to pay the penalty of having to be awake when they could have slept at ease!

I need hardly elaborate upon this historic truth. I am certain that you see at once its application to our day. We, too, are living at a signal time in Jewish history. After our people's waiting, praying and hoping for nineteen centuries, the State of Israel has been reborn. Alas, however, the enemies of Israel are still present and are threatening to destroy it. The Biblical words of God and Moses: *Heye nechonim*, "Be ye prepared!", are still ringing in our ears. And yet, alas, how many of our people are asleep in these hours when they should be awake! We need a Moses *l'oreron*, "to awaken them." Let us be awake

3. Isaiah, 50:2; Shir Hashirim Rabbah, 1:56, commenting on Song of Songs, 1:12.
4. Magen Avraham and B'er Hetev, to Shulchan Aruch, Orach Chayim, 494:3.

and let us meet the imminent challenge confronting us, lest we have to atone by enduring sleepless nights in the years to come!

And the same message comes to us as we face our religious and cultural problems today.

Here, too, the warning of God and of Moses applies to us: Be prepared! Be awake to grapple the heavy problems before us! Let us not lose the coming generation—a tragedy which threatens us. Many parents are spending sleepless nights worrying and suffering because of what has happened to their children—all because they were asleep to their duties to their sons and daughters in their waking hours.

America has given us splendid opportunities to fashion a glorious Jewish life in this country. Let us take the fullest advantage of them.

In the same Rabbinic source which I quoted from the commentaries to the Code of Jewish Law, there is included a beautiful statement in the name of the great mystic—the Ari[5]—"He who does not sleep at all in this night, *v'osek b'Torah*, and is engaged in the study and meaning of the Torah—in the message which the Torah reveals to us for our day—he may be assured that no harm will happen to him!"

---

5. R. Isaac Luria (1534-1572).

THE MIRACLE AND THE MESSAGE
OF ISRAEL'S TRIUMPH*

There is a very striking passage in one of the
Rabbinic classics of the tenth century[1], that I take
as the text for my sermon this morning: "There are
two treasures in my heart, and I have a great love
for both of them—the Torah and the people of Israel.
But I do not know *ezeh mehen kodem*, which of these
two comes first. There are people who would say that
the Torah *k'dumah*, should be my first love, and they
quote as proof the Biblical verse, 'The Lord made me
as the beginning of His way, the first of His works
of old;'[2] but I would say that my love for Israel
comes first, for it is written: 'Holy is Israel to the
Lord, the first fruit of His produce.' "[3]

This is a remarkable statement, which has special
significance for all of us today. In ordinary times
and circumstances, the Jew would not pose such a
question any more than a child would question which
of his parents he loved more; for he loved equally the
Torah and the people of Israel. Today, however, even
on this festival which marks the giving of the Torah
on Mount Sinai, all of us must say that *Yisrael kod-
min*, the people of Israel—which includes the land of
Israel—is our greater love and must be our greater
concern. For, if, Heaven forbid, our enemies had

---

* Shavuot, 1967.
1. Tana d'b' Eliyahu, chap. 14.
2. Proverbs, 8:22.
3. Jeremiah, 2:3.

[75]

triumphed, of what value would our people be, and, with our people's future lost, of what value would our Torah be?

And so, today, we come to the Synagogue, first of all, to offer our prayers of thanksgiving to God for the brilliant victory which our brave brethren in Israel achieved.

Surely, we, too, may repeat the words which the ancient Israelites sang after they safely crossed the dry path of the divided Red Sea and saw the waters covering the pursuing Egyptians: "The enemy said, I will pursue, I will overtake, I will divide the spoil . . . I will draw my sword, my hand shall destroy them . . . They sank as lead in the mighty waters . . . The earth swallowed them." [4]

Yea, what joy this victory brought to our hearts! How thankful to God we are, and how great is our pride, for the new type of Jew that Israel has revealed to the world—the reincarnation of the ancient Maccabees. Mind you, fourteen Arab nations, with a population of one hundred million people, declared war on one small land of two and a half million souls and surrounded it on all sides; they had military forces and weapons three times those possessed by Israel. Yea, a little David, standing up before the giant Goliath—and young David triumphed! How true are the words of the Psalmist which we recited this morning in the Hallel: "They surrounded me like bees, they were extinguished as a fire of thorns." [5]

4. Exodus, 15:9-12.
5. Psalms, 118:12.

And Israel achieved all this alone, without the help and without the encouragement of any other nation. Even our own beloved America did not reveal itself in the spirit of its glorious tradition. History will long remember the unworthy statement made by an official representative of our State Department, who proclaimed to the world: "We are neutral in deeds, in words and in thought!" Note well—neutral not only in deeds, and neutral not only in words, but also neutral in thought. Could anyone ever have imagined that such words would come from the lips of an official spokesman of our country's State Department! As the editor of the N. Y. Post wrote in a leading editorial: "This statement will long be remembered as one of the infamous Freudian slips made by any American diplomat in all its history."

We knew what to expect from Red Russia. In the words of Scripture: "The tents of Edom (the symbol of the red-skinned Esau—and now the true symbol of Red Russia) and the Ishmaelites (the Arabs of today) . . . they said: Come and let us cut them off from being a nation, that the name of Israel may be no more in remembrance."[6] And they remained true to their conspiratorial plans to this day. But we did expect something more from our own America. Not that we expected or wanted America to join Israel in battle. General Moshe Dayan immediately said: "We do not want America to send any soldiers here."

But we did have a right to expect that America would say to the world: "We are not neutral in

6. Ibid., 83:5, 7.

thought. We have commitments which have been proclaimed by Presidents Eisenhower, Kennedy and Johnson, to see to it that every nation in the Mid-East has a right to exist, and we shall do everything in our power, within and outside of the United Nations, to help that these rights shall be preserved!" That would have been a manly statement, which would have won the respect of most of the nations of the world.

And how great was our pride when we listened to the eloquent, brilliant, divinely inspired words which came from the lips of Abba Eban when he spoke not merely to the United Nations but also to the peoples of the world who were tuned in! The Rabbis have a beautiful comment upon the messages addressed by Moses to the Egyptian Pharaoh and also to his own people—"The Holy One, blessed be He, spoke through the throat of Moses."[7] When Abba Eban spoke, it was God speaking through his throat; it was the entire Jewish people speaking through his lips; aye, I would go further and say that it was the conscience of mankind speaking through Eban's throat.

What a contrast it was when we listened to the sleek, the sly, the brazen falsehoods of the representatives of Edom—the Russian Federenko, and his Bulgarian stooge—and of Mali—*auch a mentch*, as we say in Yiddish—a people just emerging out of savagery, who have already learned the Communist tricks of hypocritical diplomacy! I have never been so grateful for television as I was in these days, be-

---

7. Mechilta, Bachodesh, 4.

cause I am certain that the peoples of the world, just
looking at Abba Eban and at his antagonist, Federenko, could immediately sense the truth and the honesty that marked the former and the manipulated
trickery and slyness of the latter. They did not
have to listen to Federenko's words; by just looking
at his manner, at his eyes, they could see as well as
hear the falsehoods that he kept reiterating, under
the Hitler philosophy that if you repeat a lie again
and again the people will eventually believe it.

Yea, we have cause for great rejoicing. In the
words of the Psalmist, which we chanted this morning, "This is the day which the Lord hath made, let
us be glad and rejoice therein." [8] But we also must
take to heart the warning of the same Psalmist:
"And rejoice ye in trembling"[9]; or as the rabbis add:
Bemakom gilah shom t'he re'adah, "Whenever there
is rejoicing, there also should be trembling."[10] Rejoicing alone would be fatal to the present situation.
We rejoice at what happened, but we must still trem-
ble at what we shall have to face in the weeks and
months to come. And what will face us will be not
so much the schemes of the Arab rulers as those
from their masters, the communist governments—
especially Russia. Russia invested three billion dollars in arms for Egypt and Syria; and she is not
going to take their defeat lightly. She will use every
wily scheme to try to rob Israel of the fruits of its
victory. And that places a great responsibility especially upon you and me, upon all the Jews of
America.

---

8. Psalms, 118:24.
9. Ibid., 2:11.
10. Berachot, 30b.

We shall have to be, first and foremost, united as we have never been before; we shall have to set aside all the differences, the conflicts, the partisanship, that have hitherto divided us, and to become one unified American Jewry—all determined to work in behalf of Israel's future safety.

The ancient Rabbis noted that in the passage which we read in this festival's Torah lesson, telling of the wanderings of the Israelites from the shores of the Red Sea to the mountain of Sinai, where they received God's Torah, the text uses the plural, "they journeyed," "they encamped"—but when they reached Mount Sinai, the text uses the singular form, *vayichan*, "he rested opposite the mountain." "All their journeyings were marked by strife, conflict and confusion. But when they reached Sinai, all the differences were set aside and *he* rested *k'ish echad b'lev echad*, as if they were all as one man with one heart."[11] That is the first essential requirement of all Jews in America today—to stand united as one man with one heart!

The Rabbis noted something else that is strange in the wording of the sentence that I have just quoted: "And he encamped there *neged hahar*, before the mountain." [12] The word *neged* does not really mean *before* or *in front of; neged*, literally means *against, opposite*—implying opposition. And so the sages add to the scene, and connect the word *Sinai* with the word *sinah*, hatred: *Misham yardah sinah l'umot ha-olam alav.* "It was from that mountain of Sinai that *sinah*, hatred, entered into the hearts of

11. Tanchuma, Yithro, 9.
12. Exodus, 19:2.

many of the peoples of the world toward the Jew."[13] And that is the real root of Russia's hatred of the Jew. Red Russia cannot forgive the Jew for having brought down the Torah from Heaven—the Torah of truth, of justice, of mercy and love. And it is *neged*, standing against this mountain of hatred that calls for a united and unified American Jewry.

But there is also a second duty which devolves upon us if we are to prove that our love for Israel is, as it should be today, *k'dumah*—our primary love and concern. We will have to make tremendous sacrifices. Our brethren in Israel—young and old—were ready to sacrifice their lives—and many, alas, have given their lives. We are not asked to sacrifice our lives; but we are asked to give of the material resources which God has showered upon us in this land of opportunity—and to give in a spirit of sacrifice—not a pittance, not as we have given in other years.

A distinguished professor at the Jewish Theological Seminary—at the recent convention of the Rabbinical Assembly of America, which took place during the days of the Arab-Israel war—in response to an appeal in behalf of the United Jewish Appeal Emergency Fund, declared, "I give $5,000." (Professors in Jewish institutions of learning, I assure you, are not millionaires). Upon returning home he wrote to the Fund: "Here, you have all my savings, $25,000." That is the spirit of sacrifice which we must display—not to give because we are shamed by our neighbor, but to give out of a sense of duty, a sense of self-respect. We shall have to give as we

---

13. Shabbat, 89a.

have never given before—to give not only until it
hurts, but until our conscience is satisfied.

If American Jewry will stand unitedly on guard,
so that we shall not be betrayed by foe or friend, and
if we will display the sacrifices which the hour calls
for, then we will have the right to pray: "May the
Lord give strength to His people, may the Lord bless
His people with peace!"

THE UNDERLYING PHILOSOPHY OF
A JEWISH COMMUNITY COUNCIL*

Fortunately for me, I do not need to speak in my presidential message of the details of the work of our organization. Those of you who heard the very impressive report that was presented by Mr. Oscar Lewis, the chairman of our Board of Directors, know how thoroughly he covered this phase of our program. It is left for me at this point simply to summarize the underlying aspects of the philosophy of the Brooklyn Jewish Community Council, which brought about its organization just a year ago.

On the Sabbath of the week that we assembled to organize, we read in the Synagogue lesson in the Torah the chapter dealing with plagues, especially the plague of leprosy.[1] I do not know if you remember, but I then tried to analyze the whole philosophy of the Jewish attitude toward plague spots in Jewish life. I wish to continue that same discussion this morning, because it so happens that we read the same section of the Torah about two weeks ago and the story is fresh, or should be fresh, in our minds.

The rabbis ask, "How do plagues appear?" What are the causes that bring about these dangerous symptoms in our ordinary life? And the answer is,

---

* Abridged Presidential Message delivered at Second Annual Convention of the Brooklyn Jewish Community Council, May 18, 1941.
1. Leviticus, 14:1ff.

[83]

"plagues generally come *mishum tzoros eiyin*, because of trouble with one's eyesight." [2] We can understand the analysis. The ancient rabbis were also physicians in their day. Those of you who have visited the eastern lands, know how the people there suffer with their eyes. When the Zionist movement started, when you came to Palestine 40 or 50 years ago, you found three out of every four children suffering from trachoma or some other eye ailment. These rabbis accordingly felt that the eyes were the source of all the dangerous plagues that affected the people in those times.

But I think we can go a little deeper with the analysis. All plagues—spiritual plagues, moral plagues, political plagues, as well as physical plagues—emanate chiefly from faulty vision, from trouble with our eyesight, because one fails to see what is coming on. You are so blinded, your vision is so disturbed, that you do not see the first symptoms of the plague and you neglect these symptoms, with the result that gradually a plague appears that is beyond cure.

Were I to analyze the tragedy of the world today, why it is that the democratic forces find themselves with their backs to the wall, I should say just this: The great democratic governments of the world have suffered for many years from *tzoros eiyin*. They could not see what was being enacted before their very eyes. Had Great Britain and France and other democratic nations seen clearly in 1933 or in 1934 or in 1935 what was appearing upon the horizon,

---

2. Arachin, 16a. Cf. Leviticus Rabbah, 17:3; Tanchuma, Metzora 4,-*al eyin ra,* "because of poor vision."

had they not been affected with faulty vision, they would not be in their present plight. Unfortunately, they were blinded; they simply did not see. Thank God that a time finally came when they began to see, so that we may hopefully pray they can yet save democracy for the world.

And for a while it looked as if here in America too all the people were suffering from *tzoros eiyin*. You heard cries in every section of the land: "Never mind what is taking place across the ocean. Three thousand miles separate us from them. Nothing can happen with us. Nothing can harm us." The people did not see. They did not discern that these germs of hate, of destruction, and of brutality from abroad were streaming over and across the sea into the very vitals of our life. But again, we thank God, under the guidance of a clear-sighted leader, President Roosevelt, America is beginning to cure its faulty vision. It is beginning to see clearly what is happening in the world, and it is defending itself against that menace with all the force and with all the strength at its command.

Now, men and women, it may truly be said that Jewish life, too, is visited with this same tragic disease. We suffer from faulty vision; we have *tzoros eiyin;* our eyesight is blurred. We do not seem to see what is happening before our very eyes. We see the plague only when it is already here, and then we cry and shout and seek to organize to fight it. But to avert the plague when only the first germ appears—the vision needed for that we lack.

If the Jews in America had had clear vision originally, the problem of Palestine which concerns us so deeply today would not worry us as much as it does. Instead of half a million Jews, two million Jews would now have been in Palestine. The sad situation is all due to *tzoros eiyin*.

Now, to come to local matters and to our own community. Here again the same analysis applies. Why was it so easy last April to get together an enthusiastic group of men and women who came running to the first conference? Because they saw a plague which had already appeared in our communal life. In many street corners there were the followers of Father Coughlin, Christian Fronters and others who were attacking Jews and who were urging, "Don't buy from the Jews." Our people then became frightened and then got together to organize. As soon as that plague became less intense, when the danger seemed to pass, many Jews lost interest in organization. They could not seem to grasp the philosophy that the rabbis sought to impress upon us—that we have to look with clear eyes at every situation and must prevent a plague from coming into existence and that we cannot wait until the plague is here.

When we initiated the Council, I thought that most of the five or six hundred organizations in Brooklyn would flock to us and remain with us to advance Jewish communal life, to prevent plague spots from appearing in our midst. But it comes very hard. And yet, dear friends, we are not discouraged, because we realize that all beginnings are difficult and especially the beginning of the process of organizing Jewish life. It is the most difficult task that we can possibly assume. Nevertheless, we do have definite achievements to our credit.

A major accomplishment is that the Jewish people
of Brooklyn now have an address. Anyone who
wants contact with the Jewish community knows
where to apply. Previously, any petty politician, any
little man who started his apprenticeship in public
life, could purport to speak in the name of the Jewish
people. Because of chaos in our Jewish life, there
was no one to gainsay him. When government of-
ficials or agencies now want to reach the Jewish
Community of Brooklyn they know where to go—
not to an individual rabbi, not to an individual
lawyer, not to an individual judge, but to the address of the Jewish Community Council of our
Borough.

Our neighbors of other faiths also know that
this Jewish community is organized. The Catholic
Church, itself so well organized, recently needed the
cooperation of the Jews in Brooklyn. The representative of the Bishop of this Diocese came to our
Council office because he knew that it is the address
of Brooklyn Jewry. We gave the Church all the cooperation that we possibly could—cooperation that
was deeply appreciated.

Another outstanding achievement of this Council
is its program and activities in behalf of a coherent
and positive Jewish life. It is bringing order and
discipline and organization into the chaos of Jewish
life that reigned up to now in Brooklyn.

If you were to ask me for a title for this Council,
I would say that it is a Department of Sanitation in
Jewish life. It is a Department of Sanitation to
cleanse and purify Jewish communal life of all the

plague spots that have appeared and are appearing in our midst.

Our cause is worthy of an additional, high designation. The current issue of the Jewish Quarterly Review, a scholarly Jewish periodical, contains an interesting article by Professor Solomon Ganz, Professor of Mathematics at the Yeshiva College in New York, entitled "The Hall of Reckoning in Jerusalem." It is based on a certain statement of the rabbis.[3] There was a *Kipah shel cheshbonot*, a "Hall of Reckoning" outside of Jerusalem, where anyone who had an account to settle could go for a reckoning. This Hall fulfilled the verse in the Bible which said, "Jerusalem was the perfection of beauty, a joy for all the earth." [4]

Now, scholars are at variance as to the true meaning and function of this Hall of Reckoning. Some believe that it was a Department of Taxation, since the inhabitants of Jerusalem were taxed there. Professor Ganz takes issue with such view, because of the reference to the Biblical verse that Jerusalem was a joy in all the land. People are not very happy about paying taxes, and certainly a Department of Taxes would not be called the happy spot in the City's life. His theory is that the Hall watched over the economy and supervised the financial accounts of all the departments in Jerusalem to assure that there was no graft or stealing. Because it did its job so well, Jerusalem was the perfection of beauty and a joy for all the people of the earth.[5]

---

3. Echah Rabbati, II. 24
4. Lamentations, 2:15.
5. For another view, see Leo Landman, in *J.Q.R.*, Jan. 1971, pp. 199-211.

I believe there is a simpler interpretation of that Rabbinic statement. Jerusalem was fortunate in having a Hall of Reckoning where account was taken of all problems affecting the Jerusalem community; and consequently Jerusalem became the perfection of beauty, a joy to all the land.

To express in a word the underlying philosophy of the Brooklyn Jewish Community Council, I would say it is to serve as the *kipah shel cheshbonot*, the Hall of Reckoning, where it is to take constant account of the problems arising in our community and where anyone may come and ask for a reckoning of our communal life. It is a force that will bring responsibility to all the work of our communal life.

Men and women, the Council has a tremendous job. After its first year's accomplishments, I am confident that it has the possibilities to establish in Brooklyn a solid basis for fruitful and effective activity that will reflect blessedness upon its entire program and aspirations.

We have the means, we have the personnel. All we need and all that we ask now is the support, the cooperation, the encouragement of the Jews of Brooklyn. Give us that and then, with God's help, we shall be able to say of Brooklyn Jewry, as the Bible and the rabbis said of Jerusalem of old, that it is the perfection of beauty and a joy throughout all the land.

ON SERVING FIFTY YEARS
IN THE RABBINATE*

I need hardly tell you that I deeply appreciate the great honor conferred upon me in having been asked to speak at this notable occasion. I do not understand why this honor came to me. I am not the oldest in years, and certainly not the oldest in wisdom. If any one deserved this honor, it is our beloved friend, colleague and teacher, Professor Mordecai M. Kaplan, who is the *av b'shanim v'av b'hokhmoh*. But as a good soldier I accepted the assignment, and I pray to our Heavenly Father that I may prove myself able to meet the demands of this significant event.

I know that I speak for all of the rabbis who are being honored today when I say that we are deeply grateful to you for taking cognizance of the fact that we have served at least fifty years, and some of us much longer, in the American rabbinate. Having achieved this age—we must be old to have served at least fifty years—I think we have reached the stage that Lord Beaconsfield describes as the period for "reminisaging." And so I wish to reminisce with you for a little while.

It is good to recall the former years. *Z'khor y'mos olom*, "Remember the days of old,"[1] we are told. And as I like to translate the second part, *Binu sh'nos dor vodor*, "consider the *changes* of every generation."

---

* Address delivered at Convention Banquet of Rabbinical Assembly of America, in 1964, honoring the Rabbis who had served fifty years or more.
1. Deuteronomy, 32:7.

[91]

And what a change it is between the days when we were students in the Seminary and the early years of our rabbinate, and the years in which most of you were students and served as rabbis! In those early years we had no dormitory, with which you were blessed. Those of us who came from out of town especially had to search for a room in which to lodge. We had a problem of eating. I remember the hardship endured, especially for the meat meal, until finally a good, kind, old lady volunteered to cook for a small group of us. We had the same menu every day in the week, but we did not complain. We were very, very happy to get it.

When we graduated there was no Placement Commission, as there is now, to look after us. We were on our own. And there were no positions; in all the land there was just a handful of congregations. Oh, how hard it was to get a position, and what salaries, what pittances were offered! But we were glad to get them, just enough to keep body and soul together.

Often I smile when I read how young rabbis complain how hard they have to work today in the rabbinate. My dear young colleagues, we had no principals for our Hebrew schools in those years. We were the principals—in addition to preaching twice every week. In my first two positions, and even in my Brooklyn Jewish Center, I was the principal until almost my fiftieth year. And we had no executive directors, because such a creature had not even been born yet. We had to do all the work. We were the *Kol bo*. Everything, every phase of the work, had to be done by us.

When I think of what we had to do, I am reminded
of a statement in the Talmud.[2] *Anshei semonia*, the
people of the town of Semonia, came to a distinguished rabbi and said to him: *ten lonu bar nash,
sheyiye doresh, dayan, sopher, hazan, misnoyan,
v'avid kol zorkhona.* "Give us a man who will be a
preacher, a judge, a teacher of our little children, a
superintendent of our synagogue, an instructor of
our adults, one who will take care of all our needs."

That was our life in those early years of our
rabbinate. Again, when I compare our early life and
the life of the new, young rabbis, especially the
rabbis in the last two decades, I am reminded of
another statement, by Ben Zoma.[3] He compares
his life with the life of Adam, the first man on earth:
*Kamo y'gios yoga odom harishon ad she-motzo pat
lehem l'ekhol*, "How much trouble, how much labor
poor Adam had to indulge in until he found a piece
of bread to eat. He had to plow and plant and sow
and reap and grind and knead and bake," *v'ahar
kakh okhal*, "and only then did he have a piece of
bread to eat," *v'ani ashkim umotze kol dover mukhan*, "and I arise in the morning and find all prepared for me!" "And consider what Adam had to do
in order to have a garment to wear. He had to shear
the sheep and spin and weave. Only then did he have
a garment to wear, *v'ani ashkim umotze kol dover
mukhan*."

That is the difference between your generation
and our generation. You have *kol dover mukhan,*

2. Tal. Jer. Yebamot, XII:13a.
3. Berakhot, 58a.

everything prepared for you; we had to labor so hard in order to create the instruments to help us achieve results.

Worst of all, how very unprepared were the Jews in our early days for this type of Conservative rabbi. He was something new on the American scene. The people could not even understand the need for that kind of rabbi. And we had to create the demands for such a rabbi.

Today, you have Jews who want a synagogue; no matter what their motive is, they want a synagogue. As soon as they move into a community, they feel the need for a synagogue. They want their children to go to Hebrew school, and therefore they feel the need for a Hebrew school. We had to create that desire and that understanding. How I used to plead on bended knee to a parent to send his child to our Hebrew school and to join a congregation! We had to beg and beg and plead. I say to you, you have it all *mukhan!*

We speak in praise of the *halutzim* in Israel, and well we may, because they found a land that the Bible describes as *eretz asher avoneho barzel,* "a land whose stones are iron" [4]. Spiritually speaking, my dear friends, that correctly portrays Jewish life in America in the days of our early ministry. It was a soil whose stones were iron. You might ask me: *bameh heerakto yomin,* how could you live so long under those conditions, how could you survive all those years (in my case fifty-four years), how could you have endured all the hardships? I would answer

---

4. Deut., 8 :9.

in the words of the rabbis who interpreted that very text: *al tikro avoneho elo boneho*, "do not read *avoneho*, its *stones*, but *boneho*, its *builders*".[5] Its builders were of *barzel*, of iron spirit, of iron determination!

We had that spirit. We had to have it or we would have been crushed. There were other professions that offered much greater opportunities and rewards These men entered the rabbinate knowing these conditions, because they wanted to serve. They were dedicated to this ideal.

I wish to pay tribute now, and I think we ought to pay tribute, to the wives of these men, to the rebbetzins of these *halutzim* in the American rabbinate. If a young man made a sacrifice in entering the rabbinate of those years, I assure you that the young woman who married a rabbi then made a greater sacrifice. It was a greater sacrifice to be a rebbetzin in those years. All of them deserve our tribute. I know the wives of these men, practically all of them. I want to repeat a word that I used at a recent dinner with which my own Center honored me at the close of my seventy-fifth year, when I paid tribute to Mrs. Levinthal, and which I know may be applied to these rebbetzins, including Mrs. Ginzberg![5a]

In the story of Queen Esther, when she resolved to appear before King Ahasuerus to plead for her people, the Bible specifically describes the prepara-

---

5. Taanit, 4a.

5a. Wife of Professor Louis Ginzberg, who presided at the Banquet.

tions she made for that important audience. The
Bible starts the description with the words: *Vatilbash Esther malkhus*. It is usually rendered in all
English translations as "Esther garbed herself with
the garments of royalty."[6] But the Hebrew text
does not say that at all. It does not say *bigdei
malkhus*, "garments of royalty," but only *malkhus*,
which has an altogether different meaning. Esther
garbed herself with *malkhus*, the *dignity* of royalty.
Vatilbash Esther malkhus. It was the royal dignity
with which she bore herself that made the impression. And I can honestly say, not only of Mrs. Levinthal, but of all these earlier rebbetzins, that they
garbed themselves with the dignity of the royalty of
the rebbetzin. And in that way they helped us tremendously!

There is one further difference between our generation and the generation of most of you who are
here today. We had to serve the first generation of
the American immigrant Jews. They were concerned about their children, 'tis true, but they themselves still had the tradition of the Old World. Many
of them had the learning of the Old World. In my
own congregations at Petach Tikvah and at the
Brooklyn Jewish Center, I was particularly blessed
with many men who had studied in the old Yeshivot,
who were *maskilim*. They cherished and longed for
those traditions.

Most of you are serving the second generation and
even the third generation. I know one of my older
Jews who moved to a suburb and later came to visit
us. I asked him how he liked it in the new synagogue,

---

6. Esther, 5:1.

and he said, "I do not as yet feel at home there. I am the only man there with gray hair." The new congregations today consist of young people for the most part. They do not have the old learning. They want to be Jews, which is very good. But for us, forty or fifty years ago, it was a much more difficult problem.

All of my people came from congregations where they had been served by the classic type of Jewish rabbi. In my own Center it was a union between Brownsville Jews and Williamsburg Jews. Brownsville Jews were served by rabbis such as Rabbi Simon Finkelstein, *zikhrono livrokho*, the distinguished father of our distinguished Chancellor;[6a] and the Jews who came from Williamsburg also came from congregations where they had been served by the old type, classic rabbi whom I used to meet in my father's home. They knew my name and I knew their names. It wasn't easy to serve the two —the old generation of that type and the younger generation, American-born, who also came and wanted to be served.

I am reminded of a very beautiful comment that an Orthodox rabbi used at the memorial meeting for my sainted father, *zikhrono livrokho*, a few weeks after his funeral.

Since it happened to deal with the *Sidrah* of *Noah*, this rabbi quoted the first verse: *noah ish tzaddik tomim hoyoh b'dorosov*. "Noah was a righteous man, perfect in his generations."[7] "Why does the text say:

6a. Rabbi Louis Finkelstein.
7. Genesis, 6:9.

b'dorosov, in his generations, in the plural?" he asked. A man lives only in one generation. "But the text wants to tell us," he continued, "that the *tzaddik,* the real spiritual leader, must live in two generations. He must be able to talk to the young as well as to the old."

It was a beautiful interpretation, and I appreciated it when applied to my father. Those of you who knew him, know that it was true of him. I tried, and many of my colleagues tried, to follow that teaching. I never permitted myself to alienate myself from the old, though at the same time I tried to win and attract the young.

In my own case, I want to say that I won the hearts of the older generation by the Jewishness of my sermons. I did not try to compete in *halakhah* with the old rabbis of that generation, because I knew my limitations.

But my people saw in me at least a type of the old when they heard those beautiful *agadot* that God had granted me the gift of finding, and I could see the gleam in their eyes when I would give a good interpretation of a Midrashic text. In their surprise and joy, they used to go back to their old congregations and tell the old rabbis what they had heard from a young Seminary rabbi.

I won their hearts because I reattached them to the sources of their spiritual and cultural strength. And, at the same time, and this I say to you younger men, by that same method I attracted the younger generation as well. We make a mistake when we think that the young don't want that kind of teaching and preaching. They thirst and hunger for it. To them, it is the bread of their Jewish life and, alas, many of us offer them cake. They yearn for that nourishing bread.

I have had many, many experiences which proved to me the truth of that fact. Some of our men make the great mistake of dispensing with the Jewish sermon. They say we have to lecture to our people, not to sermonize; we have intellectuals, we must appeal to their minds.

Of course you have to appeal to their minds and you have to give them lectures and conduct discussions. But you have all the other days in the week for that, sufficient and appropriate time for lectures and discussions for those Jews who seek lectures. But for the vast majority, for the intellectuals as well as for the unlearned, *divrei agadot* is so important. No wonder the rabbis tell us *divrei agadot moshkhim et ha-lev*. "The Aggadic teachings of the Rabbis tend to draw the heart of man, they attract the heart" [8]; and it is through the heart that you can reach the mind, especially on the Sabbath.

On the Sabbath when the Jew has the *n'shomoh y'seiroh*, the additional soul, when he does come to the synagogue, you want to refresh that soul.

The Talmud tells us that *Rabbi Yohanan v'Resh Lakish m'ayney b'sifrei agadato b'shabbos*, "These two great rabbis, Rabbi Yohanan and Resh Lakish, would concentrate on the books of the *agadata* on the sabbath." [9] I can very well understand it. The

---

8. Shabbat, 87a.
9. Gittin, 60a.

Sabbath was the time for it, and if it was the time for the Jews of those early ages it certainly is the time for the average Jew today.

A few years ago I read in *Time* magazine an interview with the great Christian preacher, Harry Emerson Fosdick. He was celebrating his eightieth birthday at that time. The interview had dealt with various phases of his ministry, but then the reporter came to the subject of the sermon. Fosdick, as you know, was considered one of the greatest Christian preachers of his age.

The reporter asked him, "Why is it that so many people find sermons dull?" I quote now from *Time* magazine. "Dr. Fosdick offered a wise, gentle explanation of why so many sermons are boring. The business of an essay is elucidation. The business of a sermon is transformation. Some sermons are deadly dull because they are just essays on pious subjects, not sermons."

It is this very thought that the rabbis had in mind. I am convinced, and I know that all the men of my generation are convinced, that it was only through the Jewishness of the sermon that we could sense the true meaning of the words which, according to the Rabbis, God spoke to Moses: *Heheyisani bidvorekho*, "You have made Me live again through the power of your words!" [10]

You will forgive me, I trust, if I take just a few moments to give you a brief summary of a sermon I preached last Passover. I know it is rather pre-

---

10. Berakhot, 32a.

sumptuous on my part to try to preach to rabbis—
critical as they are—and rather dangerous. But I
hope that you will not think of me as a certain gentleman regarded an English Bishop, about whom
the following story is told. This Bishop liked his
food very well spiced; so he used to carry with him a
bottle of strong pepper sauce. He would not rely on
the peppers furnished in the hotel. One day as he
was sitting in the dining room of a hotel, a gentleman sitting opposite him said, "Please pass the peppers this way." The Bishop replied: "That is my
private property." "Well," said the man, "let a
fellow taste it, anyway." So the Bishop gave it to
him, and after tasting it the man said to him, "You
are a minister?" "Yes," was the immediate reply.
"And do you believe in Hell?" the man questioned
again. "I certainly do," the Bishop answered emphatically. The man looked at him and then said:
"I have met your kind before, but I never met one
who carried his samples with him!"

Please do not think of me as one who carries the
sample of his profession with him. However, I do
this because it will illustrate the thought that I am
trying to convey to you. On the seventh day of Passover I preached on the text: "Then Moses and the
children of Israel sang this song." [11] And I quoted
this beautiful and strange Midrash: *Miyon sheboro
hakodosh borukh hu es olomo*, "From the time that
God created the World" (mind you, from the beginning of time) *v'ad she-amdu yisrael al hayam*, "And
until that very day when the Israelites stood at the

---

11. Exodus, 15:1.

banks of the Red Sea," *lo motzinu she'omru shiroh*, "we do not find anyone singing before God." [12]

I put the question: "How is it possible that not one of the great men—Adam, Abraham, Isaac, Jacob—ever sang a song to God?" The Midrash even tells us that Adam was the author of the 92nd Psalm—*Mizmor shir l'yom hashabbat.*[13] So evidently he did sing.

What the rabbis meant, I thought, was that this was a different kind of song. No one before had sung such a song. It was a *shiro hadosho shibbhu g'ulim.* It was a new song that the redeemed sang.

Others had sung before, but it was an individual singing, a *shirat yahid.* An individual had it good, and so he expressed his feelings of joy in song. But here, for the first time you have a *shirat rabbim,* a whole people singing of deliverance. What a difference it makes when a whole people can sing a song of joy.

The Midrash continues: When God heard the whole people sing their song of freedom, He said: *L'eilu hoyisi m'tzapeh,* "For this I have been waiting"[14], not merely for an individual but for a whole people to sing a song of freedom!

And I developed the thought that this rabbinic comment reveals to us the true means of what we behold in today's world of revolt. Wherever you turn, you see the masses in the process of revolution.

---

12. Exodus Rabbah, 23:4.
13. Pirke R. Eliezer, 6; Genesis Rabbah, 22:28.
14. Exodus Rabbah, ibid.

What is the meaning of these revolutions among peoples long ruled by colonial powers, the revolt of the Negroes here in America, or the determined effort of the Jews in their struggle for *Eretz Yisrael*? All of these people had *y'hidim*, individuals, who were able to sing. Among the colonial peoples there were individuals who were favorites of the colonial governments, who had it very good, and who indeed could sing. Among the American Negroes there have been individuals who rose to wealth, to power, and they can sing. And even among the Jews in the Galut, there were individuals, *Hofjuden*, who were able to sing.

But now a new day is dawning. The whole group, the entire people, want to sing. They are not satisfied with their *yehidim* able to sing; they want to sing *yahad kulom*, all together, for the gift of their people's freedom.

Another Rabbi puts an additional touch to this beautiful midrash. He connects the words *oz yoshir* of our text to the words *nakhon kisakho me'oz*, "Thy throne stands firm *me'oz*, from of old," literally, "from then."[15] We usually translate the words to mean that God's throne was established from of old, from the beginning of time. But this Rabbi translates the phrase to mean: "Even though Thou art from eternity, Thy throne wast not firmly established and Thou wast not fully recognized in Thy world until *oz yashir*, until all the children of Israel were able to sing this song of freedom."

---

15. Psalms, 93:2; Exodus Rabbah, 23:1.

In these revolutions we are witnessing the eventual triumph of religion. God's throne will be firmly established, and God Himself will be fully recognized, when the purpose of these revolutions will be realized. Only then will the function of religion be fulfilled, when all the peoples of the world will be able to sing a song of freedom.

Now, my dear friends, as I told you, it was not my purpose to give you a sample of my profession. What I did want to relate was the after-effects of the sermon. After the service, the people come to you, as you know, and give you *y'yasher koakh*. Some give you a warmer one, some a cooler one. I have learned how to take these congratulatory remarks. I am my own severest critic. I know when I preach a poor sermon and I think I know when I preach a good sermon. This time, however, I was impressed. A young man came up to me, one whom I had never seen before. He introduced himself to me, and said that he was brought to the service by another congregant. I asked him his name and asked him what he did. He was a teacher of physics in a college. He congratulated me and said, "Rabbi, I want to thank you. It is the first time that I heard our ancient Rabbis having something specific to say about a problem that confronts the world today."

I appreciated that comment and I told him so. As we walked out a little later, a few others shook my hand. A young woman came to me and also gave me a warm *y'yasher koakh*. This young woman was a school teacher. She spoke practically the same words that the young man had said, though they did not know each other. "Rabbi, I want to thank you. It was so good to hear that the Rabbis of old have something to say about problems that concern us so much today."

This was the value of these rabbinic interpretations. They revitalized the message of Judaism. In my own humble way, I made the old teachings of the masters live again, and it gave the people a new respect for the teachings of these rabbis. Judaism was not then in their eyes a fossil that spoke only of thousands of years ago. It had a message for our day as well.

I must touch upon one further quality that we rabbis of the earlier years possessed. We had to possess it; otherwise we would have been spiritually frustrated. We had patience with our people. It is a quality that a true leader of his people must possess. I recall reading in the newspaper recently of a rabbi in Long Island who left the rabbinate and who, in an interview, gave the reason for his resignation from his position. He was leaving the rabbinate because, he said, it was a useless task that faced him. "I see that I cannot change the people." If that were a valid reason, the great prophets should have resigned, and Moses himself should have had to surrender his leadership. A leader must have patience with his people. No people is transformed overnight.

You have to love the people and be patient with them. Not that we did not have our moments of discouragement. We did, many a time. Not that we were not pessimistic at times. But we always remembered Ahad Ha'am's advice, "Be a pessimist for the present, but an optimist for the future!"

What preserved us and gave us strength was that we were optimists and thought of the future. We had the gift of patience which God had advised Moses to have, when he became for a moment impatient with his people: *Am zeh she'ani mosar lokh tinokos hem.* "These people whom I have entrusted in your care, they are as yet little children." *Al takpid aleihen al mah shehem osin,* "Do not become impatient; do not get angry with them on account of what they are doing. Even their Master does not become impatient with them, as it is written: For Israel is a youth and I love him!"[16] It was that quality of patience which helped us to carry on, and which can help you to carry on your duties.

Having served for fifty years and more as rabbis, we are, of course, old now. We are somewhat tired and fatigued. And yet, if you ask me whether it was worth-while, this struggle and sacrifice, let me answer your question as I answered it to my own congregation at that same dinner when they celebrated my seventy-fifth birthday. I recalled to them that there are three books in the Bible which, according to tradition, were written by King Solomon. There is *Shir Hashirim,* the Song of Songs, that beautiful song of love, perhaps the greatest love poem in all literature. There is *Mishlei,* the Book of Proverbs, the book of wisdom, in which the wise Solomon enshrined the wisdom of his rich experience. Then there is *Kohelet,* Ecclesiastes, that book of pessimism which says: *Havel havolim, hakol*

---

16. Yalkut Shimoni to Hosea, 11:1; cf. Tanhuma B'shalah, 22.

hevel, "vanity of vanities, it is all vanity" nothing is worth-while.

The rabbis add an interesting touch. They tell when Solomon wrote these books: *Shir Hashirim* he wrote when he was a young man, the time for love. *Mishlei* he wrote in middle age, when the mind is fertile and rich, and when one is able to think of words of wisdom. *Kohelet* he wrote when he was an old man, when the temptation is to say *havel havolim*, all is vanity.[17]

Judged by these standards, I honestly feel that I am not yet old. I can still appreciate *Shir Hashirim*. Thank God, my mind can still create and produce words of *Mishlei*. The very fact that on my seventy-fifth birthday I was able to publish a volume of sermons shows that God has been good to me, that my mind at least is not yet old. And, as far as *Kohelet* is concerned, I can truthfully say that I am not ready to say, *havel havolim*.

I still believe with all my heart in the worthwhileness of the Jewish life. And I still believe with all my heart in the worth-whileness of the rabbinate. I still regard it as the greatest calling that any Jew is privileged to assume. I know that I speak for all my colleagues who are honored today when I say that we all pray to our Father in Heaven that He may grant us and all our dear ones life, health and strength, so that we may be able to continue to serve our faith and our people for many, many more years to come!

---

17. Midrash Shir Hashirim, 1:10.

THE STORY OF A GREAT LOVE
and
A FASCINATING PERSONALITY*

My dear friends and colleagues on the pulpit, and my good and dear friends in the congregation!

From the depths of my heart and from the depths of the hearts of my children, we wish to thank you sincerely for this *chesed shel emet*, this genuine act of kindness, which you have shown to my cherished May, in placing on the wall of our beloved Synagogue this tablet in her memory. I feel that she is deserving of this tribute, and I am glad to see that you feel as I do.

A dramatic story is portrayed in the pages of our Bible [1] which I should like to relate to you. King David had a son whom he loved dearly. The boy became seriously ill. Throughout the illness, the King sat on the ground, refusing to eat or to talk to anyone. He prostrated himself in prayer and constantly implored Divine aid for the child. Eventually, his servants broke the news to him that his son had died. David immediately arose, washed himself, changed his garments, and ate some food.

The servants were amazed at this sudden and complete change, and they asked the King, *Mah hadavar*

---

* Address delivered on Sunday, November 20, 1966, at the Dedication of a Tablet in the Synagogue of the Brooklyn Jewish Center, in memory of May R. Levinthal.
1. II Samuel, 12:16-23.

[109]

hazeh? "What is the meaning of this change?" And
David answered, "When my child was sick, I did all
that I could to win God's favor that He should restore him to good health, but now there is nothing
more that can be done. Can I return him to life?
Ani holech elav, v'hu lo yashuv elai; I shall go to him,
but he will not return to me."

I think that I, too, can literally utter the same
words. While May was so terribly ill, we did all that
was humanly possible to win God's favor, hoping that
a miracle might occur to restore her to good health,
but God willed it otherwise. Now, like David, I can
only say "I shall go to her, but she will not return to
me."

And so, dear friends, not in mournful tones shall
I speak to you at this hour. Our very dear and devoted friend for over forty years, Rabbi Abraham
M. Heller, in his eulogy at May's funeral, eloquently
expressed our sorrowful feelings at the time. I wish,
rather, to speak to you in a very informal manner
on a subject that I would describe, "The Story of a
Great Love—and The Story of a Fascinating Personality." We all like love stories. That is why so
many are depicted in the theater; that is what at-
tracts us to novels. It is a love story that I wish to
relate to you.

The twelfth of last August would have marked
our fifty-eighth wedding anniversary. In Hebrew,
we usually designate numbers by the letters of the
alphabet. The number 58 would be written *nun ches*,
or *ches nun*. The latter form, you will note, spells
the Hebrew word *chen*—charm! This word, *chen*,
describes our love, our married life, our home; and
chen describes her personality.

May and I knew each other as young children in Philadelphia. I recall that one day, my sister, of blessed memory, speaking to her on the telephone, gave May the good news that I had put on my first pair of long pants. In those years boys did not wear long pants until their teens. May, with her usual frankness, a characteristic that marked her whole life, replied, "It's about time! He certainly needs them."

Our real attachment started later, on a day that neither of us ever forgot, March 5th, 1905. I was then seventeen years old, a senior in high school, and was quite active in "The Aids of Zion," a youth Zionist society—in fact, one of the first of such groups in the country. I was among the organizers of this group, together with other boys of Bar Mitzvah age. Each year, in order to raise a few dollars for its budget, we would arrange some sort of entertainment or concert. That year I was chairman of the concert; and I wrote to May, asking her to participate in the evening's program by playing a piano solo. She was then a student in one of the better conservatories in Philadelphia, and was known among the young folks as an excellent pianist.

The next morning May telephoned to tell me that she was sorry she could not accept my invitation. She said she had never played in public and did not think she was ready to begin. I pleaded with her and finally told her that I would call for her the evening of the concert. That evening—March 5th—I did call, and again she refused, saying that she was not ready to play before an audience. I kept urging her, and fortunately her parents came to my aid. They said, "Inasmuch as Israel called for you, you owe it to him to play." She eventually yielded and quickly changed into a simple shirt-waist and skirt. I can truthfully say, quoting the rabbis of old as they sang before the brides in Jerusalem, *lo k'chol v'lo sorak v'lo pirchus v'yaalas chen,*[2] "no paint, no powder, no hair dye and yet so beautiful,"—the beauty of youth, the beauty of innocence, and the beauty of charm.

We never forgot that evening. She performed excellently, playing Chopin's Revolutionary Etude, and she received fine applause. Every March 5th after our marriage we celebrated that event by May's playing the same Etude.

An amusing sequel was that the very next morning when she went to school her friends greeted her by saying, "We hear that you're engaged to Israel Levinthal." Evidently, those present at the concert must have seen Cupid shooting his arrows into our youthful hearts.

The following year I transferred from the University of Pennsylvania to Columbia University and simultaneously enrolled in the Jewish Theological Seminary in New York. The separation was very difficult for both of us. As the saying goes, "Distance makes the heart grow fonder," and our hearts grew fonder and fonder every day. Eventually, we decided not to wait any longer but to get married. But, as Shakespeare reminds us, "the course of true love never runs smooth"; and in our case there were many obstacles.

On both parental sides there were strong objections. My parents contended that I was too young—

_____
2. Ketubot, 17a.

I was only twenty and they argued that marriage and its responsibilities could spoil my career and prevent me from continuing my studies.

In this view they had some support from the President of the Seminary, Professor Solomon Schechter, of blessed memory. In those days the Seminary had no married students, with the exception of one older student who had enrolled as a married man. Hearing that I was planning marriage, Professor Schechter called me into his office and said, "I haven't met the young lady whom you are planning to marry, but you know what a great responsibility marriage is. You're doing well in your studies and marriage may hinder you in your work." I assured him that, although I was fully aware of the problems, I was confident that May would be of great help to me in my studies. He shook my hand and said, "I felt it my duty to talk to you, but I have faith in your judgment."

From May's parents arose a different objection— quite a serious one. May came from a home that was religiously non-observant. Those were the years, you may recall, when many of the Jewish intelligentsia were rebelling against religion. The home in which May had been reared was interested in the nationalistic and cultural aspects of Jewish life, especially in Yiddish culture, but was far removed from religious observance. Her parents did not attend synagogue worship. The Jewish community in Philadelphia was then small and everybody knew each other. Many of them felt *"es paast nit"*—it was not fitting for the son of Rabbi Levinthal, one of the leading orthodox rabbis in the country, to marry a girl from a home that was religiously so non-observ-

ant. The objection of May's parents was of equal
force. They liked me, and they told me so; but,
knowing that I was to become a rabbi, they won-
dered whether their daughter could fit into the kind
of environment it entailed. They said to her in
Yiddish, *Du legst sich mit a gesundten kopf in a
kranken bet*—"With a healthy head you're getting
into a sickbed."

Well, we finally persuaded our parents and were
married. I suppose I could stop here, echoing the
familiar saying, "They were married and lived hap-
pily ever after"; but there's so much more to tell!

We took a four-room apartment one block from
the Seminary. It was on a very fine street, 122nd
Street near Broadway. Professor Schechter and
Professor Israel Friedlander, to name but a few of
the faculty, also lived on that street. There was,
however, quite a difference between their apartment
houses and that of this newly wedded couple. Theirs
had an elevator, ours was a walk-up—and we lived
on the fourth floor. But what did stairs means to a
young couple in love, who were ecstatically happy!
We started out with very simple furnishings. All of
these, as I recall, including furniture and rugs,
could be bought for some $100 or $150; and yet,
paraphrasing the rabbinic expression, we could say:
Lo kchol vlo sorak, v'yaalas chen—"without elaborate decorations, but what beauty, what simplicity,
what charm, characterized our home!"

It was very difficult for May. Transplanted from
the only city she had ever lived in before, she hardly
knew anyone in New York. Anxious for me to succeed in my studies, she encouraged no social ac-

tivities with others. Indeed, in her eagerness to have me make the most of my time, she would quickly say if ever I wanted to indulge in small talk, "No talking! You must study! Don't talk now, because if you fail, the blame will be placed on me." She had to make good her confidence in my choice of a calling.

Our sole recreation, I recall, was the theatre. Once every great while we visited the West End Theatre on 125th Street near Broadway. Leading plays were then performed there after a run on Broadway and prior to a national tour. The gallery had no reserved seats. Immediately after supper, I would run to the theatre, stand in the usual line, and hope that for my two quarters I would get the best seats in the gallery. After washing the dishes and cleaning the kitchen, May met me at the theatre. We then did what long practice at our apartment had well fitted us for—we climbed the high stairways to the gallery. We saw outstanding performers there: E. H. Sothern, Julia Marlowe, Fritzi Scheff, among the many other great actors of that period. After the performance, we walked back to our building, got to our apartment through the customary trek, took a little bite, and washed it down with a cup of coffee. I can assure you, dear friends, with all sincerity, that the young couples today who ride to theatre in expensive automobiles, sit in boxes or in the orchestra, and then dine and dance at a fashionable night club, are not one iota happier than we were on those glorious evenings!

Professor Schechter had invited us to his home for the Sabbath meal on the first Sabbath of the school term after our marriage. I remember the awe that overcame May on that occasion. She had heard so

many admirable things about this great and picturesque sage that she was as nervous as could be
at the prospect of meeting him. Dr. Schechter, a very
humane and kindly person, and also Mrs. Schechter,
instantly made her feel at home. In turn, she capti-
vated both of them with her charm, her simplicity
and her honesty. After the meal, Dr. Schechter, who
was a prolific reader of modern literature, told her,
"I just finished a book that I liked very much. I want
to give it to you as a remembrance of our meeting."
It was Jack London's "The Call of the Wild." I
thought that this title appropriately symbolized the
gift. Evidently, he had seen the call of the wild, but
pure, love that sprang from the depths of our young
hearts.

In 1920, when I was already associated with the
Brooklyn Jewish Center, I received from the Seminary the degree of Doctor of Hebrew Literature.
Both my father and mother, of blessed memory, came
to the graduation exercises at which this degree was
conferred, just as they had come to each of four previous graduations at which I had obtained a degree
—at Columbia, at the Seminary and at New York
University Law School. During the exercises May
turned to my mother and said, "Mother, when we
married you didn't expect to see even one of Israel's
graduations and now you're at his fifth." My mother
took her hand and replied, "He owes it all to you."
She indeed uttered a very deep truth.

Mother taught May the practical procedure of
keeping a kosher home. I tried to teach her the prin-
ciples behind the laws. She was an exceedingly apt
and conscientious pupil because she wanted to ob-

serve these laws scrupulously. So faithful was she
in observance that both my mother and father had
no hesitancy in staying and eating in our home. Her
honesty in religious matters was self-evident, and
she did nothing to fail them in the least. Inherently,
she was a religious person. I had been told by friends
of the family that when she was a little girl she
would stand at the front of a downtown synagogue
on *Simchat Torah* and ask the worshippers to take
her to the services. I used to kibbitz her by saying
that the only reason I was a rabbi was that she had
been destined by Heaven to be a rebbetzin.

As she grew older, her mind developed broadly.
It became searching and challenging. With a high
sense of reason, she wanted to know the rational
basis of anything she was asked to accept or do. She
would challenge any explanation that was insufficient
or unsound. However, even though there were religious precepts that she could not rationally accept,
she observed them faithfully in deference to me. On
this point, too, I would often playfully tell her, "In
the next world you will get a double reward—one
for observing with conviction what a Jew should
observe—the second for observing without conviction, but because of your love for me."

We spent many pleasant summers at Camp Tabor
in the Poconos—later becoming Camp Ramah—in
the company of notable colleagues in the rabbinate.
After each meal we recited, together with the camp-
ers, the long *"bentchen"* or grace. One day, following a meal, May suddenly turned to the rabbis at our
table and asked, "Do you think God wants such a
lengthy thanks?" Rabbi Max Arzt, a close friend,

noted for his excellent sense of humor, answered:
"May, could you compose a shorter grace?" She said
that she thought she could, and added, "Would you
accept my version?" "Certainly," replied Dr. Arzt,
"but on one condition—it must be in Hebrew!" May
had never posed as an expert in Hebrew, and here
Dr. Arzt thought that he had trapped her. "All
right," came her instant reply, "I'll make it in
Hebrew." Swift as a flash she said, *Ribbono shel
olam, todah rabbah!* "Lord of the Universe, many
thanks." Everyone at the table applauded her quick
wit and her apt emendation of the grace. But, of
course, the routine at camp remained unchanged.

Our friends at the camp were often bewildered,
but always fascinated, by her challenging mind. Mrs.
Morris Adler, the widow of the revered Rabbi Morris
Adler, of blessed memory, who was assassinated
during a Sabbath service at his synagogue in
Detroit, once said to her, jokingly, "May, from now
on I'll call you *Rebeltzin*, not *Rebbetzin!*" May did
rebel verbally at ritual practices which she could not
rationally accept; but, out of love for her husband
and respect for her position as a rabbi's wife, she
never violated them.

During and after the Hitler holocaust, the tragedy
of the Jew had a marked effect upon her religious
philosophy. She kept challenging God, asking Him,
as had our first patriarch, Abraham, "Shall not the
judge of all the earth do justice?"[3] In many a session
with her, I tried to answer what fundamentally she
and I knew could not be answered. With her keen,
logical mind she kept searching and searching for

3. Genesis, 18:25.

an answer to man's greatest theological problem—
the problem of evil and God's justice. Like Rabbi
Levi Yitzchok of Berdichov, she summoned God to a
Din Torah—a court of law. You surely remember
that beautiful folk song which Richard Tucker and
Jan Peerce sing so feelingly in Yiddish: "I, Levi
Yitzchok, the son of Sarah, summon Thee, the Al-
mighty, to a *Din Torah! Vos host Du zu dein folk
Yisrael?*" May, too, echoed these words, "What hast
Thou against Thy people Israel?" But whereas Reb
Levi Yitzchok, after pouring out his heart in bitter
indictment, could conclude his complaint with the
words of the *kaddish, Yisgadal veyiskadash shmeh
rabba*, "magnified and sanctified be His great name,"
May could not end her plaint with these words of
utter submission.

Whenever she was in the company of rabbis or
professors she somehow turned the conversation to
that theme. I used to say to her, facetiously, "You
and Spinoza are the only God-intoxicated persons,"
for she was always searching for the meaning of
God's ways. One summer, Professor Mordecai Kaplan, whom she greatly revered and admired, upon
hearing her arguing with the rabbis on this subject,
said to her, "May, would you give me an hour of your
time and let me discuss this subject with you?"
"Gladly, Professor," she quickly responded, "and if
you can give me the answer, I shall be eternally
grateful to you." Professor Kaplan gave considerable time to expounding his philosophy on this vital
theme. When she returned to our room, she told me
that she had learned a great deal from that meeting
and that she was grateful for the wisdom that Professor Kaplan had imparted to her. "But," she added

with a smile, "Kitty dear, you need have no inferior-
ity complex." I had often told her that I was ineffec-
tive as a rabbi since I could not satisfy her quest for
an answer. "Professor Kaplan," she continued, "did
give me much to think about, but my question still
remains unanswered."

Her questioning was not marked by irreverence
or flippancy. It was rather in the spirit of the Prophet Isaiah[4] who had taught, "Seek the Lord, *b'him-
atzo*, while He may be found," a saying which she,
however, would have translated *"until you have
found Him."* If May was over-zealous in questioning God's justice, it was due in large part to her
great love for the Jewish people. It was an unbounded love that sometimes bordered on chauvin-
ism.

Whenever we entered a taxi, she would immediately examine the face of the driver as well as his
identity card posted in the cab. If she saw that he
was a Jew, she would quickly whisper to me, *Hu
shelanu,* "he is one of ours"—a hint that the tip had
to be a bit more generous than usual. When she was
in a department store, she would look for a Jewish
salesman so that he might receive the credit for the
sale. Her extreme joy on landing on the soil of
Palestine, and later of Israel, was indescribable.
How ecstatically she rejoiced when she witnessed
the remarkable and steady progress that Israel had
made between the periods of our various visits to
that Holy Land!

---

4. Isaiah, 55:5.

Many a time when we attended a large dinner affair—whether a wedding, a Bar Mitzvah, or other public function—if a cantor or layman who was to lead in the grace began singing the *Shir Hamaalot* in the melody of *Hatikvah*, May would protest, urging that this melody should be used only with the words of Israel's national anthem, and for no other purpose—not even for prayer.

Notable and dramatic evidence of her love for the Jewish people and the land of Israel was vividly displayed in the last few weeks of her final illness. She was then too weak to hold the newspaper in her hands. We therefore would tear the paper into separate pages and hold each up singly so that she could scan the headlines and signal for the next page. Whenever her eyes caught a headline that had something to do with Israel, she would point to the item and we would give her a summary of its contents. That was the only news in which she found any interest.

There was something unique in the charm of May's personality that deserves special mention. She had the gift of winning the close friendship and admiration of the wives of rabbis of the old school —women who were much her senior in age. In 1923 we visited Warsaw. I had a letter of introduction from my father, of blessed memory, to the Chief Rabbi of that city, Rabbi Kahanah, to whose home we were invited for dinner. May fascinated her hosts with her charm, her fluent Yiddish, her interesting observations of Jewish life in America, and her analysis of Jewish life as she saw it in Warsaw. Here was a young, American-born reb-

betzin in the company of a much older rebbetzin of
the old Jewish world, and yet there was instant
rapport between them. Rebbetzin Kahanah actually
fell in love with May, and, when we left, insisted
on accompanying us to our hotel. The next day she
called at our hotel to see us again and to bring May
a gift as a memento of their meeting.

In 1934 we spent considerable time in Jerusalem.
On Sabbath afternoons we were invited to tea at the
home of a close friend of my father's, Rabbi Meir
Berlin, the head of the World Mizrachi, and at the
home of Menachem Ussishkin, the noted Zionist
leader and head of the Jewish National Fund. There,
too, May immediately won the friendship of the
wives of these great men, both of whom were much
older than she and had come from an altogether
different background. That same rapport was further evident when we visited the home of the illustrious first chief rabbi of Israel, Rabbi Abraham
Isaac Kook, and his revered rebbetzin. Again there
was a study in contrasts, and yet how quickly this
young American rebbetzin won the warm regard of
this venerable rebbetzin in Jerusalem.

I am happy to add that, from the time we first
came to Brooklyn, the same relationship existed
between May and the older rebbetzins of those outstanding orthodox rabbis who adorned our community with their spiritual leadership. In the homes
of Rabbi Simon Finkelstein and Rabbi Moshe Chayim Rabinowitz in the Brownsville section, of Rabbi
Jacob Levenson and Rabbi Daniel Shapiro in our
Eastern Parkway section—each of these Rabbis and
his rebbetzin regarded May almost as a daughter.

All of them were fascinated by her charming personality. She in turn valued and cherished their warm friendship.

I could continue on and on, portraying the various facets of her personality and her activities: her endeavors in our Sisterhood, especially in its early years, when, as Chairman of the Program Committee, she did so much to improve the cultural level of the programs; her devotion and service to Hadassah and its manifold activities from the very birth of that organization; her advanced views on many social problems—she was a member of Planned Parenthood and a worker for its cause long before the movement became popular. I could also speak at great length on her extreme honesty and frankness. Often I would jestingly say to her, *Dir vet men shmeisen*—"in the other world you will be spanked, not for telling lies but for your insistence on telling the truth when tact might dictate otherwise."

I could also dwell on her great love for nature, for music and for art; on the artistic and beautifully Jewish home that she made; on her warmth and charm as a hostess to the many distinguished guests who visited and dined at our home. At a testimonial affair tendered to me in 1945, at the Brooklyn Academy of Music, at which the Jewish National Fund announced the establishment of a forest near Jerusalem to bear my name, one of the speakers was the dedicated Zionist leader, Robert Szold. In his address, he paid May a glowing tribute, saying that one of the most beautiful memories he cherished was of a Friday evening dinner at our home, where the Sabbath spirit was zealously fostered by the hostess and where her cordiality and graciousness were vividly manifested.

Above all, I could tell of the high ethical standards and spiritual ideals which she set for a rabbi and for a rabbi's wife. At a dinner we once attended in behalf of a communal cause, I sat on the dais while she was at a table with several prominent leaders of the community. A gentleman next to her, a leader in Orthodox Jewry, knowing that she was the wife of a Conservative Rabbi, facetiously asked her whether she considered herself a good rebbetzin. She immediately replied, "It depends upon what you mean by a good rebbetzin. If you have in mind one who is constantly praying and who '*shokels*' (shakes or sways) while praying, then I wouldn't give myself a high mark. But if you mean a rebbetzin who tries to live up to the highest ethical and esthetic standards befitting a rabbi's wife and, above all, one who takes good care of the rabbi and encourages him in his work, then I think I'm a very good rebbetzin."

The Talmudic quotation inscribed on this memorial tablet exemplifies in essence her concept of the ideal wife of a rabbi: "*Eshes chaver, haray hi k'chaver.*"[5] The common translation is that the wife of a scholar or rabbi is to be regarded as the scholar, that is, the same honor is to be accorded her as is due him. Her conception, however, was different and higher. She would have given a literal translation: "The wife of a scholar or rabbi—she *is to be* like the rabbi"—she is to live up to those high stand-

---

5. Aboda Zara, 39a; Shabuot, 30b.

ards of conduct and principle which one has a right
to expect from the rabbi. This teaching she tried
to uphold from the very beginning of her role as
rebbetzin some fifty-six years ago.

I have mentioned the positive aspects of her life
and character. I must, however, also tell of one fault
that she had—a fault as seen in people's eyes but
not a fault in God's eyes: she idolized her husband!
Hers was more than intense, selfless love. She
literally adored her husband.

Never would she fail to be in the synagogue to
hear me preach. As soon as I finished a sermon, her
eyes would meet mine and she would nod her head
in approval and encouragement. If I felt that my
sermon was not successful, I would shake my head
from side to side indicating my disappointment; but
she would continue to nod as if to overrule me. Sometimes, as may happen with every rabbi, I preached
an exceptionally good sermon; she would then keep
nodding her head throughout the remainder of the
service. On these occasions, when we kissed and
exchanged Sabbath greetings, she would whisper in
my ear the words of the prayer book, *En kamocha*
—"there is none like you." Though I pleaded with
her not to utter these words, telling her that many
rabbis preached excellent sermons, it was in vain.
She would continue repeating them. I finally stopped
protesting, realizing that her words were merely the
expression of her great love. Often it was embarrassing to me. In her enthusiasm, she would say to
friends who greeted us or who thanked me for the
sermon, *En kamohu*. She knew enough Hebrew to
change the phrase to "There is none like him."

Despite my pleas that she was embarrassing me, she would continue repeating her words of praise.

The last sermon that she heard me preach was on a Sabbath just two weeks before she entered the hospital for the final time. She was already ailing, and I appealed to her to stay home. I promised to repeat the sermon for her when I returned from the synagogue. But my pleading was to no avail. Though in much pain, she dragged herself to the synagogue to face me while I preached.

The Hebrew letters *nun ches* which I previously referred to, also form the Hebrew word *noch*—"to rest." After almost fifty-eight years of a blissful, married life, she went to her eternal rest. She was a realist and never feared death. Before each of the three surgical operations that she underwent during the last three years of her life—all, by coincidence, at the same season of the year—she faced hospitalization without complaint. She always expressed gratitude for having lived beyond the proverbial three score and ten years, and for the happiness and the love that she had enjoyed.

The same letters *nun ches* also form part of the root of the Hebrew word *nichem*—"to comfort." You may recall that, when Noah was born, he was given the name consisting of these two letters, because, as his father said, "This child will comfort us in our work."[6] In the midst of our sorrow, I have the consolation that our life together was a life of mutual love, truly described in the Elizabethan

_____

6. Genesis, 5:29.

phrase, "One soul in bodies twain." And I, together with my children, find comfort in the thought that hers was a blessed life of service to her people and to her fellow man, a life filled with beautiful and inspiring experiences, a life from whose heart flowed a boundless love for her family and for her people Israel. Hers was a life blessed in return by the bounteous love and devotion of her near ones and dear ones, as well as by the affection and the esteem of all who were privileged to know her.

Fervently, I pray: "May her soul be bound up in the bond of the living!"

REMINISCENCES OF A WORLD
THAT HAS PASSED—
MEMOIRS OF MY YOUTH*

Having celebrated recently the thirty-fifth anniversary of my Rabbinate at the Brooklyn Jewish Center,[1] and passing now the forty-fifth year of my ministry in Brooklyn, I have reached the age which Benjamin Disraeli characterized as *anecdotage*. I wish, therefore, to share with you some interesting recollections and reminiscences of my early youth which had a profound influence on my later life, and which at the same time may give you a picture of a world that has now gone by.

It is strange how the human mind works. Often I find it difficult to recall incidents which occurred just a short time ago, and yet I have the most vivid recollections of persons and incidents that came into my life half a century or more ago.

I really lived in two worlds then—I was part of that era which marked the mass immigration to these shores of Jews from Eastern Europe, and I shared much of the life and experiences of these people; I was also privileged to be part of that Jewish life which was totally Americanized, living and working among those who were born, reared and educated in America, and who enjoy to the fullest all that this blessed land can offer. The old Jewish

---

* These memoirs first appeared in the Brooklyn Jewish Center Review, in the issues of October 1955, and September to December 1956.
1. In 1954.

world is now gone, but it is good to recall it, to do
what the Bible so wisely advises: "Remember the
days of old, consider the years of many generations" [2]; and a wise commentator reads the Hebrew
word *sh'nos* as not *years*, but *changes*—"consider the
changes of the various generations" (attributed
to the Gaon of Wilna).

In all humility, I think I can truthfully agree
with what my distinguished brother, Judge Louis E.
Levinthal, said at my anniversary celebration—that
I am "a born Rabbi." I hope it will not be deemed
presumptuous on my part when I say that I heard
the "call" to the Rabbinate in my early childhood. It
was quite natural that I should have felt that call,
for I was not only a child of a noted Rabbi but a de-
scendant, both on my maternal and paternal sides,
of at least a dozen generations of well-known Rabbis
who had served with distinction great Jewish communities in Eastern Europe. Moreover, I had the
additional good fortune of being reared in a home
and in an environment that offered rich opportunities to come into contact with unique and outstanding personalities who had a tremendous influence in
moulding the sensitive years of my life. These were
people of high stature, of whom it could truthfully
be said: "There were giants in the land in those
days." [3]

Our home was a focal point for most of the rabbis
in the country. As soon as a rabbi arrived in America, even before he settled in any post, he would come
to our home, to get father's advice and guidance.

2. Deuteronomy, 32:7.
3. Genesis, 6:4.

There was no Jewish hotel or kosher restaurant in Philadelphia; so our home was their hotel and their restaurant. It was a veritable *hachnosas orchim*, a wayfarer's house, where a warm welcome was offered to everyone who came. I cannot recall a time when the door of the dining room was not wide open or the table-cloth was removed. A warm invitation, *"kumt essen,"* greeted all who entered. There was no formality—everything was plain and simple; yet I don't understand to this very day how my parents, of blessed memory, could have been such remarkable hosts to so many people on the pittance that was father's income in those days. Thus I had the opportunity of meeting at close range most of the rabbis and noted personalities who were to play a leading role in the development of Jewish life in America.

*   *   *

One of my earliest recollections is the first appearance in Philadelphia of the renowned Yiddish orator, Zvi Hirsh Masliansky. He had only recently arrived in America, and many of the Jews throughout the land recalled his addresses, which they had heard in the old world. His reputation preceded him, and when the report appeared that he would speak in Philadelphia the entire community eagerly awaited him. He was our houseguest of course, and we, the children, soon became attached to him. I recall the night of his talk, and though I was only seven or eight years old, I accompanied my parents and the speaker to the *Russishe Shul*, where he was to speak.

Though it was on a mid-week eve, we found the synagogue crowded to the doors. Men were standing in the aisles and on the window ledges—they even forced their way into the women's gallery. An admission fee was charged, and it is remarkable how so many of the audience who were poor paid the price so willingly in order to hear him.

For almost two hours, Masliansky held the audience in a spell. Now he would have them laughing, and a few moments later they were sobbing. He was a master at picturing scenes and in extracting new meanings from Biblical tales. Young as I then was, I not only followed his address but also was fascinated by it.

Masliansky became a frequent visitor to Philadelphia, for every organization, particularly the Zionist groups, were insistent in their invitations. I doubt that I missed any of the lectures he delivered in our city in those boyhood years, and I can truthfully say that he had a strong influence in arousing in me a love for the platform and the pulpit.

*   *   *

Nearly every *mechaber*, author of a scholarly work, seeking buyers for his book, would naturally come to our home, and father would give him a list of the leading laymen whom he could solicit and also a letter urging purchase of the book. That was the only way an author could dispose of his work, for people did not go to stores to purchase such volumes. When a very prominent scholar-author would arrive, father himself would accompany him to the outstanding laymen. The leading patron of Jewish books in Philadelphia was Judge Mayer Sulzberger, one of the famous citizens of our city, a unique and most unusual personality. He had the largest pri-

vate collection of Jewish books in all the land, and at
his death he bequeathed it to the Jewish Theological
Seminary, where it became the nucleus of the Seminary's great library today. He was the first to be approached by every writer, for it was known that he
never refused anyone and that he usually rewarded
the visitor with a handsome check.

*   *   *

About 1901, there came to Philadelphia one of the
renowned Rabbis of Eastern Europe, Rabbi Jacob
David of Slutzk, known as the *Ridvaz*, author of a
commentary on the Palestinian Talmud. His work
had been acclaimed by the Talmudic scholars of the
world, and great preparations were made by father
and the leading members of the community to receive him as befitted such a sage.

A large group of congregational leaders, dressed
in holiday attire, awaited him at the railroad station
and drove him directly to our home, where he was
houseguest for quite a long time. Of course, as soon
as he was settled, an appointment was made for him
to see Judge Sulzberger so that the judge might purchase a set of the Talmud with the Ridvaz commentary.

On such occasions, when the prospective customer
had to be addressed in English, I was drafted to act
as interpreter. And so, father, the Ridvaz and I
made our way to the Sulzberger home. We were
greeted in most hospitable fashion. The judge was a
bachelor and lived with a sister in two large houses
joined together, and the walls of most of the rooms
were stacked with books.

The Ridvaz insisted that he wanted to point out to the judge some interesting passages in his commentary, and the judge listened most attentively and respectfully. While he may have had a little understanding of Yiddish, the judge certainly could not follow the rabbi's rapid flow of interpretation. The rabbi, however, kept on—as if he were discussing the subject with another East European rabbi. Father and I became somewhat restless, but the judge displayed remarkable patience. When the rabbi had concluded the judge turned to me and, in a very gentle manner, said: "You see, my lad, no man can be great in all things." He then immediately directed his attention to the Rabbi's further comments.

*   *   *

It was during the Ridvaz's stay in our home that I was to be Bar Mitzvah, in February 1901. Many rabbis, friends and admirers of my sainted parents came to participate in this event, but I was regarded as particularly fortunate in that I would be privileged to have present at this event the great rabbi of Slutzk. My Hebrew teacher, a very learned man, taught me—as was the custom in those days—a lengthy speech, in Yiddish of course, discussing in pilpulistic fashion some intricate laws about the *tefillin*, the phylacteries, which a Bar Mitzvah lad was to begin putting on for the morning prayers.

I must confess that I do not remember now any part of that speech, and I have my doubts that I really understood then the import of what my teacher had tried to develop. The Synagogue was crowded that Sabbath with a distinguished congregation, and

I am certain that, like every Bar Mitzvah lad, I must have been extremely nervous. The Ridvaz, picturesque with his red beard and sharp blue eyes, dressed in a silk coat, ascended the pulpit first and delivered a learned address. I am sure that I could not follow its contents, but suddenly I seemed to hear him saying something similar to what I was to say in my speech. I quickly turned to my father, and in a panicky voice said: "Father, he is saying what I am to say in my speech!" But father just whispered, *"Zorg nit, du zog vos du darfst zogen,"* "don't worry; just say what you are supposed to say!"

To this day, I do not know how to explain what happened, but a beneficent angel must have guided my tongue at that hour. For when I reached the part of my speech which I heard the Ridvaz discuss, I simply added the words: *Wie der Slutzker Rav hat eich shoen gezogt . . .,* "as the Rabbi of Slutzk has already told you. . . ." These words seemed to electrify the congregation; they gave me credit for what I surely did not deserve, that I was able to follow well the *Halachic* discussion of the famous rabbi, and that I was so quick-witted as to connect my remarks with those which the Rabbi had expounded.

* * *

In 1902, an important event took place in Philadelphia, the first convention of the *Agudat Harabbanim,* the Union of Orthodox Rabbis of America. Father was the initiator and organizer of that body, and the sessions of that Convention were held in our home, where, of course, all the rabbis ate and where most of them slept. Every important orthodox

rabbi of the land was present, and I had the opportunity to know most of them. We, the children, were
quite proud of the fact that father was unanimously
chosen as the first president to head the Union.

In those years the Zionist movement was just appearing on the scene of American Jewry, and the
best of our Philadelphia Jews were already organized in an excellent Zionist group. A number of us
youngsters had also become imbued with the Zionist
ideal, and we organized the *Ozre Zion*, the Aids of
Zion, which numbered in its midst some of the finest
Jewish lads in the city. I had the honor to be the
president of the society, and when we heard that
the orthodox rabbis of the country would convene in
Philadelphia, we decided to petition the Rabbis to
formally adopt the Zionist platform. We felt that
this was an urgent step, because in those years, alas,
most of the orthodox rabbis in Europe and in
America were unfavorable to political Zionism.

As the president, I was assigned to present the
petition. The rabbis, perhaps out of respect for
father, granted me permission to appear before
them. I worked hard to prepare a few introductory
remarks before reading the petition, and I was
accorded a courteous, though I suspect not an enthusiastic, hearing. The matter, as I recall, was
diplomatically tabled, but a practical result ensued.
The next day every English newspaper in Philadelphia featured a front page story telling how a lad
of fourteen pleaded with the aged rabbis for Zionist
support.

In the following Sunday issue of the magazine
section of one of the leading papers, a long article

appeared comparing this incident with the appearance of the Christian savior in the Temple addressing the ancient sages, and the article was illustrated by the artist's drawings of the two events. If the petition had no practical effect on the rabbis, it did succeed in winning much needed propaganda for the Zionist cause.

*   *   *

One of the regular visitors to our home was the famous author of the Jewish national hymn *Hatikvah*, Naphtali Herz Imber. Whenever he came to Philadelphia, and it was most frequent, he would spend a large part of the day in our home. As soon as he entered, mother, of blessed memory, would place the whiskey bottle and glass before him and something more tangible for physical sustenance to follow.

Imber was a tragic, though colorful, figure. He was the Jewish Edgar Allan Poe—addicted to drink —and the remarkable fact was that he was most creative as poet after he had drunk his fill.

Judge Sulzberger took an interest in Imber and promised him a weekly stipend of five dollars which, in those years, was almost sufficient to supply his meagre needs. His check would arrive regularly, but it did happen at times that it was delayed. On such occasions Imber would go to the judge and in his brusque manner demand his due. Often he would insist, especially when he was not in good health, that I accompany him, which I willingly did. It was on such visits that I got to know Judge Sulzberger more intimately, and that I gained much from this contact. One of the first questions that he put to me was what I was planning to do when I grew up. I immediately told him that I hoped to study for the rabbinate, for that was my intention and ambition since early childhood. The judge then took a new interest in me. He would let Imber remain and take me on a tour among his books and show me the works of famous Jewish scholars. It was the first time that I saw ancient Hebrew manuscripts, of which the judge had quite a collection. To me, in those formative years, every such visit to this famous personality was a course in education itself, for which I am still most grateful.

*   *   *

During my early high school years, father, who was much concerned about the Jewish education of adolescent boys who had already left the *cheder*, or Hebrew school, organized the Hebrew High School, which met in our home for two or three sessions a week. He had a good group of boys to draw from— the membership of the Aids of Zion. Father himself taught us Talmud and the explanation of religious laws and customs. The remarkable liberality of my father—especially of an orthodox rabbi of that era— was shown when he invited a popular conservative rabbi of our city, Menahem Eichler, to be the instructor of Jewish history. A well-known physician and good Hebraist, Dr. Hess, was the third member of the faculty, and he taught us Hebrew. There was no tuition fee, and every member of the faculty gave his services freely. It is interesting to note that most of these young lads developed into leaders in Jewish life when they grew to manhood. Three, alas now deceased, Louis Feinberg, C. David Matt and Samuel Rabinowitz, became fine rabbis; others, like Joseph Kohn, of Philadelphia, are today leaders in work for Hebrew education, Zionism and the Synagogue.

The youthful members of the Aids of Zion—all ranging between the ages of Bar Mitzvah and fifteen or sixteen—were of an exceptionally fine type, and I must say that you rarely find such a group today. They were all imbued with a fiery devotion to Jewish culture and Jewish ideals.

*   *   *

In 1902, a noted Jewish scholar, Professor Solomon Mandelkern, died in Vienna. He had been a prolific writer and poet, and the author of the still popular Concordance of the Bible. Prof. Mandelkern had come to America a year or two before his death, and also visited our city, where the newspapers gave him considerable publicity. We youngsters certainly could not appreciate the value of his scholarship, but we had heard so much about him that when he died our Aids of Zion decided to hold a memorial meeting in tribute to him. We got permission to hold the meeting in one of the large synagogues, *Kesher Israel*, and we had the daring to call on Judge Sulzberger and invite him to be the principal speaker. The judge must have been impressed by the youthful delegation, for though he did not frequently address public meetings he readily accepted our invitation. Again I had the reward that comes with the presidency, for in that position I acted as the presiding officer.

Father was the only speaker in Yiddish; the judge and I naturally spoke in English. I displayed a weakness on that occasion characteristic of most presiding officers everywhere and at all times, in that I prepared a rather lengthy speech, evidently forgetting that the judge, and not I, was the principal speaker. The audience, however, many of whom hardly understood English, seemed nevertheless very tolerant and encouraging, evidently pleased at the sight of a young lad speaking on such an important occasion. The society later published a report of the meeting, and did me the honor of printing my address in full. I possessed a copy of this brochure until about a decade ago, when it was mislaid. I recall reading it at that time and must admit that I was rather pleased with what I had written, though it showed many marks of youthful authorship. The interesting thing about it was that this address concluded with an appropriate rabbinic quotation, which I am certain father must have given me.

*   *   *

I must tell about a unique activity of this splendid group of youngsters, in which I played an active part. The Christian missionaries had been quite active in their proselytizing efforts in the Jewish section of the city. One of the principal places of activity was on South Street, a distinctly Jewish business thoroughfare, similar to Canal or Grand Streets on the old East Side of Manhattan. We youngsters were very much concerned at the large number of Jewish children who were attracted to the Mission House by the candies and toys that were offered to induce the children to come and to join in the singing of Christian hymns and listen to Christian lessons.

We determined to attack the problem, and we did so in a very constructive manner. We organized ourselves into teams, and were assigned posts on streets. When the children were dismissed from school, each of the teams would follow a separate child to his or her home and talk with either the father or mother. In many cases, the parents were ignorant of what had been taking place in the Mission House, and instantly they withdrew the child. In some cases, our task was more difficult because the parents, who were quite poor, felt that no particular danger faced the children and were satisfied that the children got some joy from the candy or toys being distributed. We were not let down so easily, however, and would argue for days until, in some cases, we eventually persuaded the parents to keep the children away from this threat to their religious life. We did succeed in a year or two in having the Mission closed, and our Aids of Zion won the plaudits of the entire community.

*   *   *

I often think of the greatness of our ancient sages who appreciated the psychological value of merely meeting or even seeing a great personality, and who enjoined us to recite a blessing at such an experience. I had many an occasion for offering such a benediction. One of the most interesting personalities whom I had the privilege to meet was the famed scholar and rabbi, Dr. Marcus Jastrow, the author of the Dictionary of the Talmud. At the time that I first met him, he was the Rabbi Emeritus of the Reform Temple Rodef Sholom in our city. But he was of the conservative wing of the early Reform movement; indeed, he was among the early founders of the Jewish Theological Seminary. Every year, before the festival of Sukkot, he would write to father for an *ethrog* and a *lulav*. As is still the custom in orthodox circles, the rabbi is usually the one from whom the congregants obtain these Sukkot plants.

It was my annual assignment to take the plants to Dr. Jastrow. He lived in what was then the aristocratic section of far distant Germantown. I even remember to this day the exact address, 165 Upsal Street, and it would take more than an hour by trolley to get there. I even recall that on several trips I became car-sick and had to get off the trolley and wait a long time before venturing to continue the ride.

On my first visit—when I must have been no more than twelve or thirteen years old—I found Dr. Jastrow, as I was admitted to his study, working at his desk, with heavy tomes of the Talmud and other books spread before him. A large skull cap covered his head. At home I always wore a hat—to walk about or to appear bareheaded was unheard of; and so, when I entered the rabbi's study I never thought of removing my hat. Dr. Jastrow, who was then quite old, took my hand and gently advised me that it was the custom, here in America, to remove one's hat when entering a home; that only when one prayed or studied a sacred work should the head be covered.

This was my first lesson in the new ways of American religious life. But it did me no harm, for I seemed to have been more impressed and fascinated by the picture of an old sage working zealously on the old Hebrew texts. I do remember that on my return home I reported to father the lesson that I had received in the new American Jewish etiquette, but he only smiled, thinking, I assume, that I would experience many a new conflict with old Jewish folkways, and he seemed confident that I would master them.

On subsequent annual visits to Dr. Jastrow, we became much more familiar. In a fatherly way he would question me about my Hebrew and secular studies and offer encouraging words to inspire me with the will for further progress, especially in my Hebrew work. Later, at the University of Pennsylvania, where I took my freshman year of college, I was privileged to be the pupil of Professor Morris Jastrow, the son of the old rabbi, who was the head of the Semitic department and also Librarian at the University.

*   *   *

Another remarkable personality whose features and facial expressions I distinctly recall, though I saw him when I was only eight or nine years of age, was the saintly Sabato Morais, the spiritual head of the Portuguese Synagogue in Philadelphia. Twice or thrice a year, especially before an approaching holiday, this old rabbi would pay a courtesy call on father. They would sip tea and discuss current Jewish problems in which both were interested. I was too young to address him, and I suppose he must have thought that I was too young for him to speak to me. I did, however, sit and gaze at him, fascinated by his charm and manner of speaking.

*   *   *

I do not know the reason, but father thought that I should hasten my course at High School, and he arranged that I study during the summer months following my graduation from the elementary school and prepare myself for the sophomore year instead of entering as a freshman. He secured a fine young man, Albert Mordell, who himself was still a high school student, but of the upper class, to tutor me in all of the subjects of the freshman class. It was not an easy summer for me, as the courses of the Central High School, even of the first year, were of a high standard and included Latin, which was a required subject for all the four years. Fortunately, I passed the examinations in September and entered as a second year student. I attribute this achievement not to any special brilliance on my part— though I must admit that I worked extremely hard those summer months—but to the excellent tutoring that I was privileged to receive from this gifted young man who already in those years won distinction as a fine scholar. He later became one of America's leading literary critics, and we at the Brooklyn Jewish Center have had the privilege to read some of his excellent articles in our own Center *Review*.

I doubt that I would recommend parents to hasten a child's school education in this fashion.

For though the pupil may know the subjects of the year skipped, he does miss a lot of the spirit of these courses, which only a leisurely method of studying can give. Later, however, I was thankful to father and to Mordell, because this procedure enabled me to enter the Seminary and to get married a year sooner than I otherwise would. Mordell also tutored father in English in those years, and though father made excellent progress in his English studies, neither his teacher nor we, the children, ever succeeded in making him deliver a sermon or address in English; he was always fearful lest he make a mistake in pronounciation or people find fault with his accent.

*   *   *

When I was in my Junior year in High School, I decided that I ought to earn some money to help in my support, and I succeeded in getting a job as a reporter for one of Philadelphia's great newspapers, *The North American*. I was to cover the Jewish news in the city. One of my assignments which I enjoyed very much—and for which I am still grateful—was to report the Sunday sermons of Dr. Joseph Krauskopf, the rabbi of the Reform Temple Keneset Israel. He was a gifted orator who would discuss timely themes with eloquence, and he attracted overflowing congregations every Sunday.

Dr. Krauskopf was as popular among the Christians as well as among the Jews, and a large part of his weekly audience was made up of non-Jews. He would often discuss subjects that made good newspaper copy, and the editor of my paper was anxious for a regular report. Dr. Krauskopf used a flowery language and a most effective delivery. The Temple had a wide pulpit, almost like a stage, and Dr. Krauskopf would walk from one end to the other, pouring forth his thoughts. The strange thing about his speaking is that he memorized every Sunday lecture. At the Saturday morning service, when he delivered a brief sermon, he spoke extemporaneously; but the Sunday sermon was memorized.

In this temple the fine custom was adopted of publishing the Sunday address in pamphlet form and distributing it to the congregation the following week. The sexton—a Mr. Klonower—who was responsible for this publication, gave me the proof-sheets of the sermon that I was to hear; and often I would follow the text verbatim as the rabbi spoke, and would marvel at the remarkable gift that was his to memorize the sermon and yet be able to deliver it in so eloquent and effective a fashion that no one suspected that the flow of his speech was not spontaneous. I was a devout admirer of his oratory, and I would observe most attentively every nuance of his voice, his every gesture, every expression on his face.

*   *   *

One of the important events at the Central High School, which I attended, was the annual oratorical contest of both the junior and the senior years. Everyone in the class was eligible to enter the contest. An original address of about eight or ten minutes in length was first delivered at a preliminary contest, and the winners competed at a final public function in the school auditorium before a jury of outstanding citizens.

In my senior year, in 1905, I was fortunate to be selected among the small group that was to compete at the public meeting. The subject of my oration was "The Wandering Jew," in which I tried to picture the tragedy of Jewish homelessness in the last nineteen centuries and discussed the meaning of the new hope which the Jew had found in the current Zionist ideal.

This was the first time that a Jewish theme was discussed at these oratorical contests, and many of my fellow-Jewish students thought that I was rash and impolitic in choosing such a subject. Others, far better speakers than I, received the awards, but I was thankful for this rich experience in speaking before so large and so important an audience. It also gave me self-confidence, an essential prerequisite for one who aspires to speak in public. Three years later, when I was a junior at Columbia College—to which I transferred from Pennsylvania —I was chosen to participate in its annual oratorical contest and was awarded the Curtis silver medal for my address on "The Ideals of Democracy." My competitor in this contest, who won the gold medal, was Wellington Koo, who later was the Ambassador of Nationalist China to the United States.

*   *   *

I am not giving these recollections in chronological order, and so I want to go back to my earlier years at high school. It was sometime in my sophomore year that my beloved parents became concerned about my health. I was very thin and losing weight. There was in Philadelphia in those days a distinguished physician who enjoyed a national reputation, Dr. Solomon Solis-Cohen, and I was brought to him. He was one of the first Jews to serve as full professor at the famed Jefferson Medical College, and a unique personality deserving of a full biography which I hope someone will write. He was eminent in many capacities and a worthy representative of a distinguished Sephardic family. Dr. Solis-Cohen was an observant Jew, a patron of Jewish scholarship and a gifted poet. He translated a number of the beautiful poems of Jehudah Halevi, Ibn Gabirol and others of the Golden Era in Spain, and a volume of such poems—translations and original work—was later published. Dr. Solis-Cohen was a picturesque figure, and his impressive head reminded one of the portraits of a Rembrandt. He was a good speaker and I recall one of his addresses, which he delivered at an important function in father's principal synagogue, the Bnai Abraham, or "Russishe Shul," as it was known. He would have made a splendid rabbi, for he combined Jewish learning, true spirituality and deep love for God and his people. Together with Cyrus Adler and Judge Sulzberger, he was among the small group responsible for bringing Professor Solomon Schechter to America to head the reorganized Jewish Theological Seminary.

When I came to Dr. Solis-Cohen for examination he took a liking to me, especially when he learned that I aspired to be a rabbi. That won his heart at once. He examined me, prescribed certain medicine and suggested that I drink a raw egg daily. But more than that, in an authoritative voice he insisted that I see him every Sunday morning. For almost

two years, I obediently appeared in his office every
week. Though it was always filled with patients, he
gave me much time. Following the routine examination, he would start a conversation in which he
always extolled the calling of the rabbinate and
urged me to properly prepare for it. He desired to
know what I was studying and would direct my attention to books that he wished me to read. Even
after I entered the Seminary I would go to see him
whenever I came to Philadelphia. He always insisted
on giving me a physical examination and further
health directions; and then he spent equal time discussing my cultural and intellectual development. I
cannot emphasize sufficiently how much indebted I
am to this remarkable man for what he did to improve my physical health as well as for the inspiration he gave me for the rabbinic calling.

*   *   *

I think now of others who have become familiar
figures to the great mass of American Jews, but
whom I was privileged to meet in their younger
years, when they were just beginning their celebrated careers. Philadelphia was one of the first
cities in the country to develop a substantial Zionist
following. The Ohavei Zion, the first Zionist society
in the city, enlisted the intellectuals of the community, and they were enthusiastic in furthering the
cause. Mass meetings were frequently called at
which the leaders of the movement, most of whom
resided in New York, were the featured speakers.

One of the most popular of these guest speakers
was Dr. Stephen S. Wise. He was then a young man,

in his late twenties or early thirties, tall, imposing in appearance, dramatic in his oratory, and with a voice that was the envy of every other speaker. Wise was popular among the Zionists not only because of his devotion to the cause but also because he was one of the very few Reform rabbis who espoused Zionism. The Reform movement was then bitter in its denunciation of Zionism, so that Wise's adherence was all the more appreciated.

I recall quite vividly one of Wise's first appearances in our city. The meeting was held at the Musical Fund Hall, which then had the status of Carnegie Hall in New York. He was greeted vociferously by an overflowing audience. I recall that he wore a Prince Albert coat and reminded one of the handsome, popular, matinee idols of the stage.

I was very young at the time, about twelve. Not finding a seat, and not being tall enough to obstruct the view of those sitting, I stood right in front of the stage and was obliged to lift my head to get a full view of the speaker. All went well, until an usher tip-toed towards me, took me by the hand and tried to lead me away, evidently thinking that my standing there would be resented by the speaker. Dr. Wise noticed what was happening, and in his sonorous voice called to the usher: "Let the lad stand!" And then he added: "He seems more eager to hear me than some in the audience!" This remark caused laughter, and saved me from a most embarrassing situation.

I took every opportunity to hear Dr. Wise, and in later years when I was a student at the Seminary and he had founded the Free Synagogue, I was one of his attentive listeners at the Sunday morning lectures. I cherish to this day his warm friendship and the encouraging help he gave me in all the years of my rabbinate.

*   *   *

Another noted figure that I love to recall is Dr. Judah Leib Magnes. American Jewry is well familiar with the checkered career of this grand idealist and with the selfless services that he rendered to and for our people. He also was of that small band of Reform rabbis, who, in the founding years of Zionism, became one of its staunchest adherents. He, too, was a handsome figure, though not of the dramatic type as was Dr. Wise; his was the handsomeness of the sculptured Greek gods that one admired in the museums. There was a sympathetic expression on his face that just won you to him. I was so fascinated by the youthful Dr. Magnes that, when I was a student at the Seminary and saw him walking in the neighborhood, I would follow him for blocks, just staring at him.

Dr. Magnes was an orator gifted of God. It was not the dramatic oratory of Stephen Wise, but rather a soft, warm, appealing manner of speech that succeeded in penetrating the very depths of the listener's soul. Then, and especially in his later years, whether or not you were in agreement with his views, as you looked upon him you felt that you were seeing a true son of the ancient prophets of our people. I had the privilege to hear him speak at the few appearances he made in Philadelphia in my boyhood years, and also at the early Zionist Conventions—which were then not just perfunctory meetings, but rich, spiritual, soul-nourishing and heart-warming gatherings. I was blessed in enjoying his friendship throughout his life, and recall in gratitude his willingness to help me in many ways, especially in the early years of my ministry.

*   *   *

Father had been one of the original founders of the Yeshiva Rabbi Isaac Elchanan in New York in 1896, and this institution was throughout his entire life very close to his heart. Even in those early years, he would travel to New York almost every month to observe its progress and the work of its students. Until a few years before his death he served regularly as one of the examiners of the young men who were to be ordained.

On his return from one of these visits, he told the family that he had found among the young men a brilliant student whom he would like to bring to our home so that he could serve as a sort of secretary and assistant to father, and whom he wished to guide in the furtherance of his studies and career. It was not long before father did bring this young man to our home; he was Bernard Revel, who later became the head of the Yeshiva, and who was most responsible in developing this rabbinical school into the Yeshiva University.

Revel was quite young when he came to us and we, the children, soon regarded him as one of the family. He was a studious fellow, and a living challenge to us boys who enjoyed other interests besides our studies. Father encouraged Revel to perfect himself also in secular and modern Jewish scholarly studies, and was instrumental in having him enter Dropsie College, from which he was the first graduate and the first to receive the Doctor of Philosophy degree. Father, too, was the one most responsible in having him elected to the presidency of the Yeshiva. A strong friendship developed between us.

Revel was particularly fond of Mrs. Levinthal, whom he got to know in our courting days, and he was one of the group of rabbis who officiated at our marriage ceremony. Even though I went to the Seminary and he was of the Yeshiva ideology, there was no conflict marring the intimate friendship between us, and he was happy in whatever success I achieved in my rabbinic career.

*　　*　　*

There are many other recollections of my childhood and early youth that crowd my mind, but I have recorded only those which have directly or indirectly influenced my ministry. I have left for the close the memories of what were undoubtedly the greatest influence and inspiration for my sacred calling—my beloved parents, of blessed memory. I saw exemplified in their lives the highest ideals, not only of Jewish living but also of that calling which demanded a selfless dedication to all that is noblest in life.

I have mentioned a number of people from whom I learned much of the art of preaching, both from the point of view of content and of delivery. But I learned most from my sainted father. He was an extraordinary preacher, a master in interpreting the classic teachings of the ancient sages to apply to almost every problem that faces the Jew today. And while he was not a dramatic orator, he had a persuasive way of speaking, and he could hold the attention of an audience for hours by the richness of his content and the logic of his presentation. It was from him, primarily, that I acquired a great love for the treasures of our ancient Aggadic literature, as well as whatever talent I possess to draw from these classic utterances of the sages the inspiration and the lessons that I wished to bring to my people.

From the beginning of my ministry down to almost father's dying day, whenever I visited him, almost the first question that he would ask me after we greeted each other, would be, *"Host du gezogt epes gut die teg?"* This is a query difficult to translate because it implies much more than the literal meaning of the words: "Have you spoken something good lately?" He meant, of course: had I given a new, a novel, a worth-while interpretation of a Biblical or Rabbinic teaching? And when I repeated to him a sermonic thought based on a new insight into a classic text—which I was sometimes fortunate to achieve—his eyes would suddenly sparkle and his exclamation, *"dos is gut"*, "that is good," was the greatest reward that I could hope for, and always a stimulant for further mastery of the preacher's art.

*   *   *

The world that I have tried to portray, and nearly all of the great personalities who helped to mould

Jewish life in that world, are now gone. But I have indeed been fortunate to be part of that world. When I think of those spiritual giants who then lived and whom I was privileged to know, I can repeat the words of the liturgist: "Happy is the eye that has seen all this!" The sages of the Talmud have a beautiful saying which applies to older people reviewing their early life: *ashre yaldusenu shelo beeshoh es ziknusenu,* "Happy is our youth which has not put to shame our old age." [4] Having already entered the years of *ziknah,* of aging, I can repeat these words of the rabbis, and add: "Happy indeed is a youth such as mine that has so enriched and blessed my advancing years of life!"

*   *   *

In an earlier part of these reminiscences I recalled the personalities and events of my early childhood and youth which had greatly influenced me in choosing the rabbinate as my life career and had developed in me a love for and an appreciation of the art of preaching. I wish now to record the Jewish life in my home city of Philadelphia in those days more than sixty years ago.

It is strange how vividly such early memories come back to one. And the older one gets the more does the mind insist on recalling the past. When we are young we live in the future, in dreams and hopes of what is to be. When we begin to feel the approach of old age the process is reversed. Instead of living in the future we instinctively relive the past. The wise rabbi tells us: *Ben shishim l'ziknah,* "At sixty

---

4. Sukkah, 53a.

one reaches old age"; *ben shivim l'sevah,* "at seventy, the hoary head." [4a] But the Hebrew expressions are much more meaningful. One does not always become an old man at sixty. The rabbi does not say, "at sixty one is a *zaken,* an old man." He says, "at sixty *l'ziknah,* one goes towards old age." And so, too, "at seventy, *l'sevah,* one goes towards the hoary head." We may still cling to youth, and even at times deceive ourselves into believing that we are still young. But these memories of the past, which begin to force their attention upon us, are ample proof that we are going *l'ziknah,* towards old age.

* * *

The earliest recollections that I have are of the *cheder,* the Hebrew school, which I attended. There was already in those early years a *Talmud Torah,* a community Hebrew school, which my sainted father, of blessed memory, had succeeded in founding. It was situated, as I recall, on Catherine near Third Street. Why I was not taken to this school I do not exactly know. The reason may have been that just because it was a community school no tuition fees were charged. In fact, the English name of the school was The Hebrew Free School. And so those who could afford to pay and those who, though they could not afford it, wanted to pay, sent their children to a private school or *cheder.* I was taken to such a school, conducted by a popular teacher, a Mr. Sheftelson.

In keeping with the old tradition, my sainted mother, of blessed memory, brought me to the *cheder*

4a. Abot, 5 :24.

when I was about six years old. The very first day of a child in the *cheder* was most memorable, and it must have made an indelible impression on the young mind. Before the child had had a chance to accustom himself to his new surroundings, the teacher immediately initiated him into his studies. The teacher would show him the Hebrew alphabet and mechanically make him repeat the sounds of the letters and the vowel points.

As the child succeeded in repeating a few of the letters, and while his eyes were glued on the page, the teacher would let fall a penny and some sweet cookies, informing the child that this was a gift dropped by a heavenly angel, rewarding him for his interest in his studies. I recall such a scene vividly, though I cannot vouch that this recollection is of my own initiation. But it happened so often—with the registration of each new pupil—that it seems as if I myself had received those heavenly gifts.

The teacher was rather odd in appearance, resembling one of the Pickwickian characters. He was short and stout, with a big, round head, without beard or mustache. Not that he shaved, but hair just did not grow on his face. The entire *cheder* consisted of one large room on the second floor of his home. He was the sole teacher, and he had a rather clever system. There were three or four rows of benches. Each row represented a group or a class. In the first row sat the youngest children, then came the next older group, and finally there was the row of the oldest boys. (The entire student body consisted of boys, since no one at that time thought it proper or necessary to send girls to a *cheder*.)

While Mr. Sheftelson taught one row, the others would study their lesson. He then proceeded to the next row and, while he taught it, his eyes would continually rove over the entire class, instantly spotting a pupil whose attention had wandered. Usually he sat at his desk while teaching and sipped from a glass of milk and hot water which his wife or dutiful daughter would continually bring to him.

On a conspicuous part of the front wall of the classroom, a leather strap hung which served as a constant warning to us. The strap was far from being an ornament. Many and many a time it would be used in a manner which of course would not be tolerated today. If a boy wilfully disobeyed an order, if he could not account for an unexcused absence, or, if for any reason, in the sole judgment of the teacher, he was deserving of punishment, he would be asked to step forward, to lie down on the front bench and, while two older boys held him in that position, the strap began its work—without hindrance from the victim's pants. The strange thing to note is that seldom would the boys complain of this treatment to their parents. It was accepted as a norm in the process of education. And even if a boy did complain to his parents, he received no sympathy, the usual retort of the parents being that if he had been punished he undoubtedly had deserved it.

*   *   *

But there were also times of unbounded joy in the *cheder*. The festival of Hanukkah was one such occasion. Weeks before the approach of the festival, the teacher would shop for toys to be presented to the pupils. The classroom was a veritable toy-shop, stuffed with sleds, police and firemen's suits, and all sorts of games. The teacher would write the names of all the pupils on slips of paper and place them into a bowl. In another bowl he would set the slip on which he listed all the gifts. On Hanukkah, a party was arranged, at which the slips of both bowls were drawn, and the prizes were awarded according to the reading of the slips. Everyone seemed satisfied and happy with whatever chance accorded to him, and the spirit of Hanukkah joy was an unforgettable one.

Despite the fact that the school session consisted of three hours, five days a week, I must confess that the amount of knowledge the boys acquired after several years of study was very elementary—a familiarity with the prayer book and the mechanical translation of certain sections of the Pentateuch. In fact, when I was about nine or ten years old, father transferred me to another *cheder*, conducted by a well-known teacher, a Mr. Hoffman, where the curriculum was more advanced. While beginners were admitted, these were very few, and most of the boys would study the Prophets and Psalms, the commentary of Rashi, and even the beginnings of Talmud.

Mr. Hoffman was a handsome man, tall, with a fine, dark brown beard, and possessing a rare capacity for making the pupil study. It was he who prepared me for the Bar Mitzvah ceremony. He, too, was the sole teacher of his school, and the method of instruction was similar to that of Mr. Sheftelson.

Whether the child learned much or little, the teachers of both schools somehow did succeed in instilling a love for the Jewish people and a reverence for our religious teachings and ideals. I recall one afternoon in Mr. Sheftelson's school when the entire class had gathered, awaiting the entrance of the teacher. When he entered, even the youngest child could sense that he was deeply depressed. We missed the customary jovial greeting. Taking his seat, he turned to the class and in a tone of sadness said: "Children, a great tragedy has befallen our people. The Rabbi of Kovno, Rabbi Isaac Elchanan, died!" In a few simple words, of Yiddish, the language of instruction, which all the boys understood, he told of the Rabbi's greatness and of his undisputed leadership of world Jewry.

I was then very young, about eight years, and though I and the other youngsters could not fully appreciate the meaning of the announcement, all of us, nevertheless, were made to feel that something terrible had happened to our people, and a peculiar sadness filled our hearts the rest of that day. I remember that when I came home I found father saddened by the same news, and he was rather pleased that our teacher had told us of the enormity of that loss.

In my high school years I no longer attended *cheder*, but was given instruction at home. I was fortunate in those years to study under three masterful pedagogues—Mr. Baruch Hanapolsky, who became the first principal of the Yeshivah Mishkan Israel, Mr. Hillel Malachovsky, one of the pioneers in publishing a fine children's Hebrew textbook for Bible study, and Mr. Joseph Doktorowitz, who had won fame because of a beautiful model of the ancient

Temple in Jerusalem which he had constructed with remarkable skill, and which was often exhibited in Philadelphia and New York. One of the great joys of my life was that Mr. Malachovsky and Mr. Doktorowitz, who later made their homes in Brooklyn, became frequent worshippers at the Brooklyn Jewish Center and listened to the preaching of their former pupil. It is difficult to describe the tender feelings that were mine when I preached with these men before me and when, after services, I received their warm congratulations and frequent, rich suggestions.

*   *   *

A few weeks after the death of the great Rabbi of Kovno, father announced that he would deliver a *hesped*, a eulogy of the deceased, on a certain evening in the Bnai Abraham Synagogue on Lombard near Fifth Street. It was his custom to offer such a *hesped* on the death of every outstanding, rabbinic scholar. But here there was special reason—the Rabbi of Kovno had given father *semichah*, rabbinic ordination.

Young child as I was, I accompanied father to this memorial meeting. The synagogue was crowded long before the announced hour. Many of the Jews of that day had only recently come to America. The name of Rabbi Isaac Elchanan, as well as the names of the other great spiritual leaders in the East European lands, were familiar to all of these Jews. They knew of their greatness, and their death struck at their hearts as if someone very close and dear to them had passed away.

The *hesped* in those days was altogether different
from the formal eulogy of our time. Father first
went into a learned discussion of the important role
the scholarly leader played in Jewish life and of the
rabbinic evaluations of such a loss, and then, coming
to the immediate subject of the eulogy, he would
begin in a most plaintive, sing-song manner, to describe the depth of the loss. The entire congregation,
men as well as women, would join in uncontrolled
sobbing. As a climax, father would suddenly turn to
the ark, unfold the ark cover, and, with the entire
congregation standing, plead to our Heavenly
Father, in the same plaintive voice, to spare the
people another like loss and to continue to bless them
with spiritual and scholarly leadership.

Such a *hesped* usually lasted about two hours, concluding with the Cantor's chanting of the *El Moleh
Rachamim* prayer. While the congregants became
exhausted because of the sobbing and the emotional
strain, they nevertheless felt a peculiar satisfaction
in having participated in a loving and reverent
tribute to one whose services they appreciated so
much. They did not hurry from the Synagogue; they
wished to linger on and on, as if they could not
sufficiently express their great sense of mourning.
Alas, how rare now is that feeling of personal attachment to the spiritual and cultural giants of our
day! Now, I must state that while I have these
definite impressions of father's *hesped*, I cannot
vouch that it was the *hesped* for the Rabbi of Kovno
that I have just described. Father was frequently
called upon to deliver such *hespedim*, and it is possible that, having heard him so often when I was
older, I may have subconsciously associated these

memories with that early event. And yet, the fact keeps repeating in my mind that it was just that important *hesped* that I recall.

*   *   *

Since I am not recording these reminiscences in chronological sequence, I return to my first Hebrew teacher, Mr. Sheftelson. Once a year, he played an altogether different role. It was the custom for the leading laymen of the various congregations ministered to by father to assemble in our home on the afternoon of Shemini Atzeret (the Festival of Conclusion following Sukkot) to welcome in happy and joyous fashion the festival of Simchat Torah—the Rejoicing of the Torah. Long tables, laden with food, beer, wine and whiskey, filled the large dining room, office and parlor.

At such a gathering it was permissible, nay, almost mandatory, for even the most sedate and formal of Jews to get into the spirit of the day and to abandon themselves to the fullest measure of joy. They would dance around the tables, singing traditional melodies, exalting the glories of Torah. At every such celebration, Mr. Sheftelson was the leading entertainer. He would suddenly change character, wrap his head and face in a woman's shawl, and impersonate an old woman as she read her *Tezenah Urenah,* the popular Yiddish folk collection of Biblical tales and their simple interpretations which pious women loved to read on the Sabbath. It was more a caricature than a portrayal, and, because his beardless face could be made to resemble a woman's, his impersonation would cause unbounded laughter. And yet it is strange, and certainly true of the traditional Jewish character, that though there had been merriment and the strong drink had had its usual effect, the fun would suddenly stop and all would turn to father with the request for "a word of Torah"—which was but another, and perhaps a more beautiful, way of asking him to deliver an address.

The spirit immediately changed; the address was not a venture into humor at all, but rather a serious dissertation on the importance of Torah in Jewish life and how the joy of Torah should really express itself. It was only after the address, to which the assembled guests listened with great attentiveness and admiration, that the entire company, with father at the head, proceeded, in gleeful fashion, to the synagogue, there to participate in the procession of the Torah scrolls and to give full expression once more to their great delight in the Torah.

*   *   *

In recalling such joyous gatherings, I turn to a festive occasion which was annually celebrated by the Philadelphia Zionists. These were an enthusiastic group which took advantage of every opportunity to instill a love for the Zionist ideal in the hearts of our people.

As the reader undoubtedly knows, all our major festivals are of both a religious and national character. These Zionists succeeded in restoring and re-emphasizing the national aspect of holidays which retained in the diaspora a purely religious character. Such a festival—a minor one indeed—was Hoshanah Rabbah—the seventh day of Sukkot. According to a folk tradition, the final fate of man for the coming year is sealed on that day. Though the Day of Atonement is deemed to be the final day of reckoning, the people's mind fashioned this extra period to give the sinner one more chance to win God's favor.

Thus the custom developed among pious Jews of remaining awake the entire night to recite portions of the Bible and special penitential prayers; for the heavens were supposed to open that night so that the prayers could more easily penetrate the portals of the throne of Heavenly Justice.

The Zionists made use of this day of grace by annually reserving Hoshanah Rabbah eve for a Zionist gathering. Here, too, they would sit at tables, piled with fruit and goodies prepared by the wives who, although not yet organized into a separate women's society, were so imbued with the Zionist ideal as to be always ready to do their share in furthering the cause. The people would assemble and begin the celebrations at a late hour, after ten o'clock, since they wished to continue the festivities till long after midnight.

Many of us youngsters, members of the "Aids of Zion," would also participate, and, after the gathering disbanded about two in the morning, we would always resolve to stay awake the remainder of the night. We would take walks or stop for coffee at the Horn and Hardart Automat, on Eighth and Chestnut Streets, but finally, despite our good intentions, we had to give up and return to our homes for at least a few hours of sleep.

This annual celebration had a tremendous influence in strengthening the Zionists' idealism and their dedication to the cause. They would look forward all year to this event, for they felt that on that night they acquired what the pious Jew achieved on the Sabbath, a *neshamah yeserah*, an additional soul, which granted them a double share of devotion to their people and to their people's old-new land.

*   *   *

Social gatherings were utilized by the Zionists constantly for effective propaganda purposes. Our "Aids of Zion" and the companion girls' organization, "Daughters of Zion"—both made up of zealous and enthusiastic youngsters—also adopted this procedure to win additional members for our groups. Concerts, dances, raffles and other such means were frequently used.

One such social gathering, a musical evening, of which I was chairman of the arrangements committee, left an indelible impression on my mind—and for a very good reason, as the reader will soon realize. This happened a few years later than the incidents previously described. In fact, the date—March 5, 1905—has become a memorable one for me.

I knew for a number of years a young girl, very pretty, who loved the piano, and whom—though I was no musician at all—I knew to be a good pianist. As chairman of the committee, I invited her to play a solo that evening. She declined, for she was too shy to play in public. But I was persistent. I told her that I would not take "No" for the answer and that I would call for her the evening of the affair. I did call and succeeded in persuading her to come with me.

In gallant fashion, I introduced Miss May Bog-
danoff who would play for us a Chopin waltz. The
audience responded to her rendition most appreci-
atively, and applauded for an encore, which she
gave. The interesting fact to note was that the very
next morning at high school both this girl's friends
and my friends came to each of us to tell us that they
understood we were engaged. They did not guess
wrongly, for that date marked the real beginning
of a lovely friendship which culminated in a blessed
union. To this day,[5] we gratefully celebrate the date
of March 5 and listen with great pleasure and fondest memories to her playing once more that same
waltz of Chopin's.

*　　*　　*

I keep wandering in my memories. My mind goes
back now several years, when I was much younger,
in order to portray the way of life of many of the
Jews of the community at that time. We must remember that most or nearly all of the Jews living in
the southern section of the city—the real Jewish
section—had but recently immigrated to America.
Even most of the young people of that day had been
born in the East European lands. They had brought
with them the European pattern of Jewish life, its
folkways and thoughts, and these reflected themselves in many ways.

Atlantic City was then—as it is now—a popular
summer resort for our people, and I remember that,
when I was quite young, father and mother and the
children would spend several weeks at the resort.

---

5. This was written before her demise on May 26, 1966.

The folks not only loved ocean bathing but also had the belief, quite current then, that salt-water bathing had a curative effect on almost everything that ailed one.

I need hardly remind the reader of the type of bathing suit in vogue fifty or sixty years ago. The men wore long bathing shirts with sleeves, and trunks that covered the ankles; the women displayed full blouses and long skirts and stockings. Quite a number of the Jews could not reconcile themselves to the idea of a rabbi's appearing in a bathing suit on a public beach—and, even worse, bathing at the same time and in the same place that women were bathing.

In the downtown streets of Philadelphia, the report made the rounds, *der Rov bodt sich mit veiber.* "The Rabbi is bathing together with women!"

Of course, many saw the humor in the complaint, but to quite a number this kind of mixed bathing seemed incongruous and out of keeping with rabbinic behavior. Father took no note at all of these complaints and continued his usual procedure of ocean bathing. Saintly mother, however, took it to heart. She was very sensitive to possible criticism and always went out of her way to avoid the slightest cause for faultfinding. In fact, that was one theme she tried to impress upon us, her children—that just because our father was a rabbi we had to be especially good, since anything unworthy of us would reflect upon him. It actually pained her to hear the criticism of father's bathing, and I am sure she lost much of the pleasure of the family's ocean visits.

And so, when father was making his way into the water, ducking the waves, mother would summon us to stand guard around him, to serve as a protective wall and to see to it that no woman *chas v' sholom* (heaven forbid) should come near him. For, strange as it may seem, there were women who, either because they did not know of the criticism or because they saw nothing wrong in such action, would actually come close to father as he waded in, to give him a friendly welcome and the encouragement to "come in, the water is warm!" Mother was always ready to marshal the children when she noticed the approach of such a friendly female.

But folk habits and ideas do give way to newer concepts with which they come to clash; and, within a year or so, all talk about father and mixed bathing disappeared, and mother could enjoy her ocean bathing fully.

*   *   *

Although mother, of blessed memory, passed away more than twenty-five years ago, I am certain that many of my readers still remember her and that those who do will recall her saintly character and unique personality. She was a *Rebbetzin* by birth, brought up in Wilna, the daughter of one of the rabbis who served as *Dayan* (Rabbinic adjudicator of Jewish law) in that historic city. She had a high conception of the rabbinate, and felt that the wife of a rabbi had to sacrifice her individual life for the people of the community; they had to be made happy, they had to be made to feel that they and their welfare were her concern.

Consequently, friendliness, above all, was the major characteristic of my mother's personality. When anyone entered our home—the ringing of the bell was unnecessary since the front door was always open—whether he was a friend or a stranger, mother always greeted him with a warmth that instantly made him feel at home. *"Vos macht ihr?"* ("How are you?"), was her immediate greeting. *"Vos macht euer veib und kinderlach?"* ("How are your wife and children?"), she would continue, taking a chance that the stranger had a wife and children. And if we would tease her by saying that the man might not be married, she would merely reply: "Well, God willing, he will have a wife and children." And, whether it was mealtime or long after, invariably came another question: "Have you already eaten?" The person did not have to say no, but a mere gesture would instantly prompt her to insist that he sit down at the dining room table to partake of some food that was brought for him.

Remarkable patience was also one of mother's traits—especially in relation to my father. She would never interfere in his work or in what he felt to be his duty, no matter how it inconvenienced her. Father was never a man of routine; he was unable to follow a set hour for his meals. Often he would be in his study talking to people, the hour for lunch having long passed. Mother would then enter and ask him to please "come to eat." He would reply, "In a moment," but a half hour would pass, and he would continue his conversation. The same procedure would be repeated several times before the session ended and he finally came for his meal. Even then, if one entered during his lunch and needed advice or an answer to a question, father would not permit the visitor to wait for him but would leave the table. While this must have placed a strain on mother, she never lost her patience—though in later years she would mildly complain. As a matter of fact, I never remember mother showing any evidence of anger. When she did feel irritated she would walk about humming a melody, and when we heard her doing this we knew that something had displeased or hurt her.

Mother had a fine sense of humor. I remember that when we visited my parents during the summer in Atlantic City and went for a stroll on the board-walk, father and I would generally walk together, discussing things of mutual interest, while mother and my wife would walk together following us. Father was so well known by the promenading people that again and again they would point to him or turn to give him an extra glance. *"A behr geht,"* ("A bear is walking"), mother would jokingly re-mark to her daughter-in-law, as if the people's star-ing reminded her of stares caused by an unusual sight. Her sense of humor and her readiness to smile served her well in the difficult conditions of the rab-binate, especially in the early decades of their rab-binic experience.

* * *

Of the almost anarchic conditions in the religious life of the Jewish community in Philadelphia more than half a century ago, the following incident is a good illustration. From the very beginning of his rabbinate, father had tried hard to bring some order into the chaotic situation that existed in the field of *kashrut*. He finally succeeded, with the help of the leading representatives of the orthodox congregations, in organizing a city *Vaad Ha-kashrut* to supervise the slaughterhouses and the stores that claimed they sold *kosher* meat. *Mashgichim*, or supervisors, were engaged whose duty was to visit these stores at will and examine the meat sold. If unfavorable evidence was found, or if there was cause for suspicion, the butcher was summoned to see father who discussed the evidence with him and warned him to be more careful. When these warnings were disregarded, father would have a statement posted on the bulletin board of every synagogue, announcing that this butcher and his store were no longer under the *Kashrut* supervision and that observant Jews should therefore refrain from patronizing them.

One butcher who was thus penalized determined to challenge the authority which the rabbi and the organization had assumed. On a certain Friday, late in the afternoon, when we were already beginning to prepare for the Sabbath, a sheriff's assistant appeared and handed father a warrant for arrest on the ground of criminal libel. The butcher had deliberately arranged for the warrant to be served on Friday late afternoon, so that father would not be able to supply the necessary bail and thus be forced to spend the Sabbath in jail. Father had to think quickly. I remember that I was rushed to a dear friend of father's—Mr. Benjamin Finberg, a successful real estate broker on Walnut Street—to urge his immediate help. Mr. Finberg instantly accompanied me home, and as soon as he heard what had happened he took the sheriff's representative aside, whispered, took something from his pocket and shook the man's hand. The warrant was served next Monday. That Sabbath afternoon father was scheduled to preach at the Kesher Israel Synagogue on Lombard near Fourth Street.

I should note that in those years as well as until recently sermons were not preached during the Sabbath morning service, but in the afternoon, preceding the *Minchah* prayer. The sermon then was not just a twenty- or thirty-minute interpretation of the weekly portion of the Torah but a learned disputation of Jewish law which the Torah portion had inspired. It lasted an hour, and often much longer, and only towards the end would it present some appropriate lesson for the needs of the day.

The sermon at that time appealed to the learned among the laymen, who enjoyed this intellectual reminder of the intricacies of the law which they once had learned. Many who were not so versed also heard father's sermons because he had the true preacher's gift of popularizing even the most difficult theme. It must also be noted that sermons were not preached on a regular weekly schedule. Whenever father thought it necessary, whenever he had something urgent to say, he would have a regular printed form posted on the synagogue wall announcing that on that Sabbath afternoon, at a specified hour, he would deliver a sermon in this or that synagogue. For, being the rabbi of most of the congregations, father would arrange to preach in all of them in rotating fashion.

The news of the attempted arrest of father quickly spread among the worshippers in all the synagogues that Sabbath morning. We were therefore not at all surprised to find the synagogue filled to overflowing long before the scheduled hour for the sermon. All this happened when I was only about fifteen, but I still remember father's opening and rather dramatic sentence: "Here stands before you on this Sabbath *an arrestant*," a rather difficult word to translate into English, for it implies one arrested because of a criminal act. With fine oratorical skill, he portrayed the chaos existing in the Jewish communal life and the need for religious organization and discipline and, above all, for the recognition of religious authority which, in the old world, had preserved our religious way of life.

The case of the Butcher vs. the Rabbi became the *cause célèbre* of the year, and the English press featured it in all details. Christians as well as Jews became interested in its outcome, but it actually never came to trial. The butcher evidently could not stand the shame and censure that were heaped upon him from all sides, and he withdrew the complaint.

* * *

Father's leadership and constructive work were beginning to be appreciated by the mass of his congregants. When my youngest brother, Cyrus, was born, the leaders of the various congregations participated in the festivities of his *Brit milah*. Indeed, all family celebrations were then community celebrations, and this event was no exception. Leading rabbis and prominent leaders from other cities also came to honor our parents. And of course speeches were the main order of the day on all such occasions. The great and popular orator, Rev. Zvi Masliansky, a devoted friend of the family, was also present, and all were eager to hear him. As a climax of his address, he suggested that those present give evidence of their appreciation of father's service by purchasing and presenting to him a home.

This was a novel idea in those years, indeed, the first such instance on record among the orthodox Jews in this land. The proposal met with hearty approval, and instantly the responses came in rapid succession. Several thousand dollars were there and then pledged. At the same time a committee was formed to bring the proposal to the entire community, so that the necessary sum could be secured. It did not take long before the spacious house at 716 Pine Street was purchased. The dedication services which marked the family's entrance to their new abode lasted an entire week, and the leading rabbis of the country took part in the different programs arranged for each day of that week. It was in this house that father and mother spent the major portion of their lives, a house which has become a familiar and an almost historic landmark in the life of Philadelphia Jewry.

*   *   *

One of the very important functions of the traditional rabbi was to adjudicate legal disputes that arose between people. It was not regarded fitting for Jews to go to civil courts to settle such disputes. Jewish law was still recognized as the valid authority to guide people in all differences, in family matters and business relationships. In fact the disputants could choose whether they wanted to have the decision be strictly according to the Talmud and

Choshen Mishpat — the section of the *Shulchan Aruch* (Code of Jewish Law) — or to rely on father's personal judgment as an arbiter of the case. His clear judgment in analyzing the differences in the disputants' claims, his logical thinking and his mastery of Jewish jurisprudence quickly won for him such high reputation that hardly a week passed without people's coming to him for a *Din Torah*—a Jewish adjudication of their difficulties. These were not always small or petty cases. Often they dealt with claims involving many thousands of dollars. But there were also unique, almost freakish, cases. One deserves to be retold.

The daughter of a prominent, orthodox rabbi in New York—whose reputation for learning and piety was known throughout the land—was married to a young rabbi, the son of another well-known rabbi in a large western city. I deliberately refrain from mentioning their names because of the oddities of the situation, though I am certain a number of the older people of Philadelphia still remember the details. The marriage had been arranged by friends of both parties. One of the conditions of the union which the groom had insisted on was that the bride promise to put on a *sheitel*, or peruke, immediately after the ceremony. The groom was very pious and felt this was essential for his wife's salvation and for his own happiness. The bride, who, it must be admitted, was no longer young, readily agreed to this provision.

The marriage took place, and although weeks passed the wife did not keep her promise but gave plausible excuses. Finally, the husband suspected she had no intention of acquiring a *sheitel*. He left her and insisted on a divorce. By mutual consent, they agreed to bring the case before father.

I remember the long sessions which lasted for days and into the nights. What impressed me then, though I was still young, was that the wife's father, a venerable rabbi with a long, yellow beard, known as an uncompromising fighter for the established orthodox regime, was a pleader in behalf of his daughter. "Such a beautiful head of hair to be shorn? What impudence to demand it!" he kept shouting. It must be admitted that though the wife-defendant could not participate in a beauty contest, the one attractive feature she did possess was beautiful, blond hair. But the correct way for a pious woman to wear the *sheitel* was to have all her hair shorn before she affixed it on her head. This same rabbi, who was very intimate with our family and who of course stayed in our home during the hearings, approached me one morning, stroked his palm over my cheek, and questioned me: *"Yisrael, du razirt sich?"* ("Israel, do you shave?"). I recall my embarrassment, for I had just begun to shave my adolescent hair growth. Shamefacedly, I had to admit my guilt, and I know that he must have been keenly disappointed with me.

Father kept arguing with each side to give in for the sake of *shalom bayit*—the preservation of family peace—but both parties remained adamant. He postponed rendering a decision several times and each time made them return to their homes, hoping that meanwhile they would find a solution. I am sorry that I do not remember how the matter was settled, for after one such postponement they never returned for the verdict. I have a feeling that both parties began to realize that father was stalling and that they would have to make their own decision.

* * *

Father was a staunch believer in the value of Jewish education and the importance of every cultural endeavor in behalf of the young and old. He was convinced that if there was a future for Jewish life in the new American environment it could be safeguarded only through a knowledge and an appreciation of the Jewish cultural and spiritual heritage. I have already mentioned the Talmud Torah which he had been influential in organizing. So, too, in later years, he founded a more advanced school for boys who graduated from the *Talmud Torah*— the *Yeshivah Mishkan Israel.* There was at that time a Hebrew Sunday School Society, organized among the German Jews to establish Sunday Schools for the benefit of boys who did not attend a daily Hebrew School, and especially for girls who had no opportunity to receive a Jewish education. These were to gather for a few hours on Sunday morning for instruction in Jewish history and religion. I recall two such schools, one at the Touro Educational Building, on Tenth and Carpenter Streets, and one in a hall, usually used for weddings and social gatherings, on Eighth Street, between Lombard and South.

Though such schools offered a minimal educational program, and though their sponsors were of the up-town, German-Jewish element, father gave them his blessing and encouragement. He was very happy when both my sister and I volunteered to be teachers in one of these schools. He would often tell us what we should teach, and he was always interested in hearing of the progress we were making. Particularly gratified was he that these schools attracted large numbers of girls as pupils. He realized that the community was not yet ready to understand the need for intensive Hebrew education of girls, and he was glad that these Sunday Schools were making a beginning in moulding Jewish opinion towards a realization of this great necessity. Sister Lena, still remembered by many Philadelphians though she died when quite young, was thirteen months older than I. She never went to a *cheder*, but was one of the first group of students at Gratz College (then in its infancy), and therefore was qualified to instruct young children.

We taught at the Eighth Street school, and though all the classes met on the one floor in the large hall—and there must have been several hundred children—the order and discipline were perfect. This testified to the interest of the children, the devotion of the teachers, all volunteers, and particularly to the ability of the principal—a Miss Newhouse, as I recall, a most capable pedagogue and an intensely faithful Jewess. The principal would invite speakers to address the entire school during the assembly period at the close of the session. Often she would also arrange to have some of the teachers deliver these addresses. I recall the joy I derived from having received such invitations several times, for they gave me an opportunity to speak to an audience, an experience I have always appreciated.

As this was a modern school, conducted by those long Americanized, it was not required that boys keep their heads covered during the sessions. Hebrew not being taught, this did not become an issue, and some wore their hats while many did not. The speakers who addressed the assembly, as I recall, always stood with head uncovered. I remember the advice which father had given me when I was preparing my first address there, "When you mention the name of God cover your head with your hands." And then he told me that that was the custom of the sainted Sabatai Morais, the beloved spiritual leader of the Portuguese Congregation Mikveh Israel, when he appeared on an occasion which required his speaking with uncovered head. I followed father's advice, and recall that my action won the approval of the principal.

*   *   *

Gratz College, too, received father's enthusiastic support and cooperation, though it represented an innovation in the field of Jewish education unknown at that time in the East European lands. Its purpose was to offer young people of high school and college age who never had had any Jewish instruction a systematic modern education in Hebrew and in Jewish history and religion. I recall the frequent visits to our home of the Rev. Henry Speaker, the devoted principal of the college, and Arthur Dembitz, the instructor in history and one of the most lovable personalities one could possibly meet. They would discuss with father the program and the needs of the school and especially the ways and means of attracting the young people as students.

Every opportunity that came to father to educate the Jews was eagerly grasped by him, for he was convinced that in education alone lay the hope for a meaningful Jewish life in America. The idea of a Friday night lecture series, such as is in vogue today in many synagogues, was totally unknown among the Jews who had recently immigrated to this country; but father quickly realized that Friday nights, after the Sabbath meal, could be utilized to spread a knowledge of the Jewish past and Jewish ideals among the masses who had had no opportunity to learn or to study.

The Touro Hall of the Hebrew Educational Building was a large and spacious auditorium, and father got permission to use it for a series of Friday lectures during the entire winter months. These were not sermons that he delivered, though at times, when special occasions or needs arose, he did utilize the sermonic approach; they were lectures in the truest sense of the term, in which he discussed the lives of the great heroes, prophets and sages who had fashioned Jewish life, the important historic events, and the greatness and uniqueness of the teachings of the Bible and the Talmud. Though Touro Hall was not in the heart of the Jewish section—in fact it was quite a distance from it—the auditorium was filled every Friday night with men—and even some women —all eager for Jewish knowledge. There was no religious service in connection with the meeting, but only the address, which lasted at least an hour. This was not an easy assignment for father, for he was usually exhausted by his heavy week-day burdens; and to make matters worse, it was a long distance to walk from our home to Tenth and Carpenter Streets, particiularly when the weather was very cold, or when it rained or snowed. But neither weariness nor weather ever kept him from appearing for his address.

* * *

One of the children usually accompanied father to these lectures. But the one who was always with him was his *shamash*, Mr. Isaac Matt, a tall, picturesque figure with little eyes, thick eye-glasses and a long, heavy, brown beard. The word *shamash*, used in this case, is difficult to translate. Literally, it means a *servant*. But that would do an injustice to him and to the relationship between him and father. "Aide" and "assistant" are truer definitions of the word. It was the tradition in the old Jewish world that a rabbi should have a *shamash* always at his side. Mr. Matt served in that capacity for father ever since I can remember; I imagine he took this role as soon as father came to Philadelphia in 1891. He accompanied father wherever he had to go—to visit the slaughter houses, to attend meetings, to deliver sermons or lectures. Anywhere and everywhere father went, Mr. Matt was always sure to go.

It was Mr. Matt who would deliver the summons to a person called for a *Din Torah*, or who would attend to the arrangements if a *get* (divorce) proceeding had to be conducted. He was also with father at every wedding ceremony, for it was he who saw to it that the *chupah* was in order, that the glass for breaking and the proper wine were on hand; and above all he was there so that father could be assured of having always at least one pious Jew as a witness to the *ketubah*, or marriage contract. He seemed to be ever present at our home—early morning he would be there, and if father was busy with people until late at night Mr. Matt would not leave him. All of us at home regarded him as one of the household, and we could not visualize our home without him. *Reb Isaac* was the way all of us addressed him —father, mother as well as the children; and it was by that name that everyone knew him. His son David, who was about my age, was one of my earliest and closest friends throughout all my childhood and adolescent years; we went together to *cheder*, to high school, and to the Hebrew high school which father had organized, and we were both among the founders of the Aids of Zion. He, too, entered the rabbinate, having graduated from the Jewish Theological Seminary, and he served with devotion and ability several important congregations, including the West Philadelphia Jewish Community Center. Alas, he died in the very midst of his fruitful career.

Reb Isaac would not tolerate the slightest disrespect to father. I recall several instances when father had to scold a butcher who had been summoned before him because of improper adherence to the *Kashrut* regulations; and when, in the heated arguments that followed, the butcher would begin to speak in a tone which Reb Isaac thought was not sufficiently respectful, he would unceremoniously grab him by the back of his neck and literally throw him out of the house. We children nicknamed him "the constable," for that described part of his duties. If any of us children misbehaved and had to be punished, it was not father or mother who assumed the unpleasant duty. In fact, I cannot remember any time when either of our parents punished us. It was always: *"Reb Isaac, shmeist ihm un"*—"Reb

Isaac, give him a licking!"; and Reb Isaac would dutifully undo his belt and tenderly simulate a beating, for he loved all of us even as his own children.

I was reminded of Reb Isaac when I spoke of father's Friday night lectures. In walking from our home to Touro Hall, we had to pass a section, thickly populated by recent Italian immigrants. The present Inter-Faith movement was then unknown, and the sight of a Jew, especially one with a long beard, was sufficient cause for an outburst of "sheeny" or just the hissing sound *"biz!"* Father and Reb Isaac ignored these insults. But when snow covered the ground, these loafers—as we called them —were not content with just calling names but indulged themselves in the fine sport of aiming snowballs at our heads, and particularly at Reb Isaac's long beard. But they had not reckoned with Reb Isaac. He would chase them, and when he succeeded in catching one, he would give him such an unexpected thrashing that never again would the lad throw a snowball at him. The whole gang got to know this bearded Jew and feared him. Gradually the trip became a safe one, and we even received smiling greetings from many of the people as we passed them. We got our first lesson in how to meet the challenge of such budding Jew-haters.

*   *   *

Another cultural effort of those days deserves recalling. A group of the intellectuals among immigrant Jews organized what was called the Hebrew Literature Society. A building was secured, also on Catherine near Third Street, and there they established a library of Yiddish, Hebrew and English books, organized discussion groups and started weekly lectures.

That was the era when the intellectuals rebelled at all tradition; religion to them was outmoded; socialism was the coming gospel that would save the world. Most of those who led in these cultural ventures were of this school. The themes of most of the lectures dealt with the new economic, political and social theories. Discussions would follow the lectures, and these were marked by an intensity and argumentative heat befitting zealots of any cause.

Strange as it may seem, father too was invited to participate in one of these lecture series. He knew that it meant a Daniel's entering the lions' den—for, to these people, a rabbi was the defender of an outmoded past, while they were the apostles of the new truth. Father unhesitatingly accepted the invitation. He announced as his subject, "Labor Laws in the Talmud." This lecture attracted a record-breaking attendance. For almost two hours father brilliantly expounded the views of the Talmudic sages on the pressing problems in which these intellectuals were interested; he opened a new world before his audience, and prolonged applause was his reward. And then the question and discussion period began. The zealots of the new philosophy kept hurling questions and took issue with some of the speaker's interpretations. But father held his ground, and for another hour he answered questions and criticism.

The result of that appearance was that the invitation was repeated annually, and for a number of years his lectures dealing with the classic Jewish views on many of the current problems became the outstanding feature in the program of this society. It is interesting that despite the disparity in views between father's and those of many of the leaders of these intellectuals, father gradually won their friendship, and a number of them became frequent visitors to our home. Father certainly did not believe in the isolationist policy now in vogue in large circles of the orthodox groups. It was his deep conviction that all Jews, of whatever view or opinion, are brothers, that a spiritual leader must endeavor to win them, not to eliminate them, and that the way to win them was through understanding, tolerance, patience, and, above all, instruction.

*   *   *

In a previous part of these reminiscences I referred to Dr. Joseph Krauskopf, the gifted rabbi of the Reform Temple Keneset Israel, in Philadelphia. He was a dynamic personality, a man of tremendous energy and great organizing ability. In 1904 he presented a report at a meeting of the Central Conference of American Rabbis held in Louisville, in which he pleaded for the establishment of Reform congregations in the sections of the cities inhabited by the East European Jews. He was a staunch believer in Reform Judaism and wished to spread its doctrines among those still under the influence of Orthodoxy.

In the summer of that year, he succeeded in organizing such a Reform congregation in the downtown section of Philadelphia. The group rented a hall on Fourth and Bainbridge Streets, in the very heart of the Ghetto section similar to Hester or Rivington Streets on the East Side of New York, and announced that the Southern Jewish Reform Congregation would hold services there on the High Holy Days. The announcement immediately caused an uproar among the orthodox Jews of that section. The orthodox rabbis and the lay leaders of the orthodox synagogues issued a circular, which was widely distributed, announcing to the Jews "that the place at 422 Bainbridge Street, which is advertised as a place of prayer for the High Holy Days is not a Synagogue but a strict Reform place, which is organized by the missionary labors of the Reform Union," and urging them not to worship in those premises.

I am indebted to Mr. Maxwell Whiteman—assistant to Professor Jacob R. Marcus, Director of the American Jewish Archives in Cincinnati—who is working on a history of the early Jewish settlement in Philadelphia, for recently calling to my attention a letter which I then wrote to the *Jewish Exponent*, the Anglo-Jewish weekly in Philadelphia, dealing with this very project. Another correspondent of the *Exponent*, who signed his letter "Fair Play," had denounced the opposition of the orthodox leaders and particularly the circular which they had issued. "It became evident," he had written, "that some of our brethren who fled here from Europe to obtain freedom of worship and freedom of speech have not yet learned that they must allow the same freedom to others. . . . To attack a religious movement by claiming that it is opposed to religion must be a new form of wit. For it has absolutely no meaning unless the writer meant that reform was opposed to a

religion of many prayers and few deeds. So it is."
And continuing in this vein, "Fair Play" had concluded his letter with this sentence: "When it came
to signing the circular, courage must have failed
the perpetrators, for it bears only the legend 'The
Committee.' "

Mr. Whiteman was kind enough to send me pho-
tostatic copies of the above letter, of the Yiddish
circular, and of my letter, which appeared in the
Exponent in the following issue (September 14,
1904). On reading that letter now, I must state that
I marvel, first of all, at my audacity—I was sixteen
and a half then—in plunging into this affray. Despite the length of the letter, I think that it is worth-
while to reproduce it in full:

"Editor of *The Jewish Exponent*. Sir: I read with
much interest the very curious and rather amusing
correspondence that appeared in your columns last
week under the heading of 'Campaign Methods in
Religion,' and signed 'Fair Play.' I will endeavor to
the best of my ability to answer each and every
argument presented by 'Fair Play.'

"First, he writes that a Yiddish paper has given
the movement its support. He refers to a New York
Yiddish daily that printed in its advertisement columns an advertisement of the organization. They
would receive the support of many other Yiddish
papers, if they would only visit their advertising
agents in Philadelphia.

"He is then surprised that his brethren (?), who
fled here from Europe to obtain freedom of worship
and freedom of speech, have not yet learned that they

must allow the same freedom to others. I would like to ask 'Fair Play' if he has ever seen any such circular printed against the reform temples in the upper section of the city? Why, of course not! They have a right to worship and to speak as they will. But when you send missionaries to our Ghetto to enlighten us, here where we are interested, may we not have something to say on the subject? After all, we are not idol or totem worshippers. We really have a religion, a strange religion, perhaps, but still a religion. And it is called Judaism. We believe that this entitles us to an opinion on the subject. We also believe that we ought to be consulted. (Incidentally —but, of course, that doesn't matter to folks who need to be uplifted by missionaries—we are insulted.)

" 'Reform is a religion of many deeds and few prayers!' he then writes. Their many deeds are to doubt and deny the inspiration of the Bible, to kick over every symbol and trample it under foot, to sneer at every ceremony, to ignore our history, to abandon all we have suffered during centuries of martyrdom. Those are their many deeds. That's enlightened; that's modern; that's what is called being 'reformed.' And that is the gospel which these missionaries wish to preach to us, who are old-fashioned, not enlightened, because we are orthodox —that is, we are Jewish Jews.

"I am greatly in doubt if 'Fair Play' has visited the charitable and educational institutions of the Ghetto that are supported by the 'Sh'nai Shillings' that the poor orthodox Jew, who peddles all day long with a heavy pack on his back, donates at the Torah

reading on a Sabbath. If he would visit the Home
for Hebrew Orphans, where nearly one hundred
homeless and fatherless children find a home, if he
would visit the Mount Sinai Hospital, where thousands of poor Jews are treated free of charge, the
Talmud Torahs, where nearly one thousand children
get a free training in Jewish history and literature,
the Sheltering Home, where hundreds of Jews, who
immediately on reaching our shores, find free shel-
ter, and the many other institutions of the Ghetto,
all of which are supported by poor orthodox Jews, he
would find out which is a religion of many deeds.
And yet, 'orthodoxy,' says he, 'is a religion of many
prayers and little deeds.' Orthodoxy tells us to care
for our downtrodden brethren. You will find thousands of orthodox Jews interested in Zionism, which
seeks for a future for the persecuted Jew. The re-
formers do not care to try to better the condition of
their brethren. And yet, orthodoxy is a religion of
little deeds, and reform of many deeds.

" 'Fair Play' also writes that the issuing of this
circular was fit for corrupt politics, and not for
religious questions. But I would like to ask 'Fair
Play,' what is more corrupt, and what is more fit in
corrupt politics: Whether to fool a people by issuing a poster informing them of the organization of
a 'Southern Jewish Congregation' (eliminating the
word reform), or to tell the truth to a public, which
has been fooled, that it is not a Jewish synagogue,
but a reform temple? I leave it to your readers.

"His meanest attack was made upon our holiest
institution — the Cheder. Without going into a
lengthy discussion of the Cheder, permit me to inform 'Fair Play' that those reform rabbis who pos-

sess even the most meagre Hebrew education obtained it not from the religious school of the Temple,
but from the Cheder. So far, having seen many
graduates of religious schools, I have not found one
who is able to read a Hebrew sentence without
'N'kudos' correctly. If 'Fair Play' would visit the
Yeshiba Mishkan Israel of Philadelphia, where over
fifty boys study the Talmud, and if he would see the
respect that is paid to their teachers, he would
readily find out from where we can expect the future
generation, whether from the religious school or
from the Cheder.

"Now that I have answered every one of his arguments, I would like to ask 'Fair Play' what does the
Southern Jewish Congregation wish? They know
very well that those who are inclined to reform
would not fear lest they are 'M'chalel Shabos,' and
would ride to the up-town temples where they could
hear excellent choirs and great orators, see magnificent buildings, etc. Those who have declared themselves atheists and are opposed to orthodox Judaism
will surely not go over to this service. But what
bothers them is this: If a child who had the mis-
fortune to work on the Sabbath, and could not attend
the synagogue, and for once in a year, on Rosh
Hashana and Yom Kippur, his father can have him
at his side at the service, where he is at least reminded that he is a Jew, we have missionaries sent
to us to take away the opportunity from the parent,
to tear the child from the parent's breast and to
teach him a religion which is opposed to his parents'
religion.

"I am greatly surprised that 'Fair Play' did not
practice what he preached when he wrote that cour-

age must have failed them because they merely
signed 'The Committee,' and he himself had not the
courage of his conviction to sign his own name. I
wish to inform him that in their case, not as in his
own, it was not the lack of courage, but there were
many names to sign, as the committee consisted of
all the orthodox rabbis of Philadelphia, and of all
the presidents and prominent members of all the
downtown congregations.

—Israel Herbert Levinthal
Philadelphia, September 14, 1904."

Whether these arguments would have validity
today, or whether I would offer such arguments
today, is not the question. The reader must remember that this happened 52 years ago, when most
Philadelphia Jews downtown had but recently arrived in America and held fast to the traditional
Jewish life which they had brought with them from
the old world.

The congregation did hold services on the High
Holy Days and on Sukkot, at which Rabbi George
Zepin, the national director of synagogue extension
work of the Union of American Hebrew Congregations, officiated. I recall attending one of the services
on Sukkot, when Dr. Krauskopf himself came down
to preach the sermon. Dr. Krauskopf knew that
this congregation was different from his own Temple
congregation, that many of these Jews still appreciated a word from the classic Jewish texts. And I
even remember the text that he chose—the beautiful
passage in the Midrash in which the ancient sages
tell us that the four Sukkot plants resembled important parts of the human body—the *ethrog* or

citron, the human heart; the *lulav* or palm branch, the backbone; the leaf of the myrtle branch, the human eye; and the leaf of the willow branch, the human lips. The sermon did make a great impression upon the congregation, and I have no doubt that were he the regular preacher the movement might have made considerable progress.

As it was, the efforts of this group were unsuccessful. The congregation did engage a spiritual leader, Rabbi Max Raisin, a young graduate of the Hebrew Union College. But though the movement was financed by the two prominent Reform Temples, Keneset Israel and Rodef Shalom, it failed to influence the Jews of the downtown section. After struggling to keep the congregation going, it soon failed to attract worshippers at the Sabbath service, and within seven or eight months the entire project collapsed.

*   *   *

I have now concluded these few vignettes of a Jewish community life in an American city, that has long passed and that is now only a memory. I wish to return to several incidents in my own personal life, which also reflect a world gone by.

As I have already described, I became engaged to the girl who was to become my beloved wife, soon after my graduation from High School. I took my freshman year of college studies at the University of Pennsylvania, but before the end of that year I became anxious to hasten my course of studies so that I could sooner marry. I determined to make an effort to be accepted as a student at the Jewish Theological Seminary, for I had never departed from my ambition to become a rabbi.

I must mention now a fact which may come as a surprise to many a reader: in that ambition I received no encouragement from my father. Though he was eager that I master as much Jewish learning as possible, he was not at all anxious that I take the rabbinate as a career. The position of the orthodox rabbi throughout the country in those years was a frightful one, full of hardships and difficulties. Though the Yeshiva Rabbi Isaac Elchanan was already in existence—father having been one of its founders—it was then but a replica of the old European *yeshivot*, and a far cry from the Yeshiva University of today. The whole concept of "modern" orthodoxy was then unknown.

The idea of Conservative Judaism was still in a nebulous state, and at that time could not have won the whole-hearted approval of father. The future of the Seminary itself was yet unknown, for its reorganization, under the leadership of Solomon Schechter, of blessed memory, had taken place only four years before I entered as a student in 1906. The Seminary too, was then under severe attack from many of the old, orthodox rabbinic leaders, for to them any change in the East European concept of a rabbi was an attack upon the traditional Jewish life. Father, having won recognition as a national leader among the orthodox rabbis, would thus be placed in a difficult predicament if his son were to become a student at the Seminary.

The reader can therefore understand and appreciate why father was not enthusiastic about the rabbinate as a career for me. He preferred that I study for the law, a profession which my three brothers had entered, and for which my one sister too had studied. Indeed, when I was younger, he would often send me with messages to a well-known lawyer, Mr. Bernard Harris, one of the few East European Jews to have achieved success in the legal profession in those early years, hoping that I would become fascinated by his achievement and follow his career. I have a feeling that these errands were pre-arranged, for Mr. Harris took much time at every such visit to discuss my future, to suggest good books for me to read, and always to tell me the advantages of the legal profession. But these visits made no impression upon me, and the very next Sabbath I would listen to one of the English-speaking rabbis and return home all aglow with the desire to some day occupy a pulpit.

Nevertheless, father finally adjusted himself to the inevitable and yielded to my desires. An interview was arranged with Professor Schechter, to which father accompanied me. We met at Professor Schechter's home, and he greeted us with a warm welcome. Before he even began to discuss my problem, he entered into a lengthy conversation with father, and I quickly saw that both were very much impressed with each other. And then the talk turned to me. Professor Schechter questioned me in detail about my Jewish and secular studies; and here instantly I encountered a major obstacle. The by-laws of the Seminary provided that the applicant for admission as a student had to have the equivalent of a Bachelor of Arts degree. That degree is, of course, conferred at the completion of a college course of study. I was then finishing my freshman year at Pennsylvania. Among the papers that I had brought with me, and which I showed the professor, was my

High School diploma. But something unusual occurred which, like a beneficent angel, saved me in my dilemma.

The Central High School is the only high school, or certainly one of the very few, in all the land that confers upon the graduates of its classical course the Bachelor of Arts degree. It had been endowed with this right by the State Legislature more than a century ago, and it still follows all the formalities of that academic procedure.

Of course, that degree has no practical value, as the school's graduates must take the full course at college in order to receive the college baccalaureate. But it saved my situation. Professor Schechter agreed to accept this technical B.A. conferred on me as a compliance with the by-law provision, with the understanding that while taking my studies in the Rabbinic Department I would manage to arrange for courses to be taken at Columbia and thus to receive the college degree before my graduation as Rabbi. I enthusiastically agreed to that condition, and in fact that very summer I took as many courses as permitted in the Summer School at Pennsylvania for extra credits, and managed to get the B.A. at Columbia in January 1909, a year and a half before my graduation from the Seminary.

I recall an interesting plea that Professor Schechter made to me at the conclusion of that interview, a plea which I am sure he made to every incoming student. "Don't be satisfied with emulating the American rabbi whose fame rests on his oratorical abilities and pastoral duties alone. Make every effort always to gain more Jewish knowledge, and

REMINISCENCES OF A WORLD THAT HAS PASSED

try to make some contribution to Jewish scholarship!" He then pointed, as examples of what he meant, to a long list of British, Christian clergymen who fulfilled all the duties required of clerics and who still were able to make notable contributions in various fields of scholarship. I am afraid that I disappointed him in this regard. Dr. Schechter, evidently, did not yet realize the heavy and at times unbearable responsibilities, as well as manifold duties, that were to occupy the attention of the rabbi all the hours of the day, especially in those pioneering years. Already an ancient rabbi had complained that he had forgotten sixty important laws which he had learned from his great teacher because he was so deeply occupied *b'tzorche tzibbur*, with the needs of the community.[6] Nevertheless, the admonition which Professor Schechter gave me at this first interview never left me, and it remained before my mind as a living challenge to what I ought to aspire. I tried hard to remain faithful to that ideal and, for a while, after publishing my thesis on the Jewish Law of Agency, I maintained a studious interest in that field of comparative jurisprudence. My only modest contributions in later years, however, were my books of sermons and discourses, in which I did endeavor to present in popular fashion the great and imperishable ideals of our people.

* * *

I have often asked myself why this special privilege of admission had been accorded to me. I certainly had not possessed an exceptional amount of Jewish learning, especially in comparison with that

_____

6. Tanchuma, Voera, 5.

of the students whom I met in the classroom. Most of them were much older and were stocked with Talmudic learning which they had brought with them from the European *Yeshivot*. But it must be remembered that the Seminary, as well as the re-form and orthodox schools, had very few students; the modern rabbinate was not at all then a popular profession, and Professor Schechter was anxious to secure students, especially among those reared in the American environment.

I have a suspicion, too, that there may have been also a subconscious desire on the part of the pro-fessor to name among the students the son of one of the leading orthodox rabbis in the country. That would indeed be an effective diplomatic answer to the steady attacks which were being hurled not only at the Seminary but also at its new head.

The fierceness of those attacks cannot be imagined by the American Jew of today. I recall one of these biting assaults, which was supposed to be very clever and which made the rounds among many of the orthodox groups. The leading Yiddish newspaper of that time was the *Tageblatt* or *Jewish Daily News*. It became the mouthpiece of the orthodox, since the readers to whom it catered were mostly of that group. One of its important and popular writers was Professor Getzel Zelikovitch—he always ap-pended that title to his name, for it gave him added distinction among the readers.

In the first years of Professor Schechter's leader-ship of the Seminary, this writer became the leading propagandist of the group which persisted in at-tacking him. Around Passover time, when the Seder Haggadah was fresh in the reader's mind, Zelikovitch played on the paragraph in the *Chad Gadya* tale which says: *V'oso ha-shochet v'shochat hatoro,* "the slaughterer came and slaughtered the ox," and made the pun: "And Schechter (literally, the Yiddish for *slaughterer*) came and slaughtered the Torah" (the sound of the word *toro* being similar to that of *Torah*). Such was the virulence of the attacks in those years which Schechter had to meet.

To be able to announce that a son of one of the outstanding orthodox rabbis was a student at the Seminary was indeed a fine victory for Dr. Schechter. And I may state now that father faced many an uncomfortable hour in having to answer for this surrender of his son to the ranks of the enemy. As I look back on the years of my ministry, I do not think that father was ever disappointed with the step which I then took.

* * *

It was not an easy task that I faced. The Seminary course alone would have been a sufficient challenge to me—for, as I have already mentioned, most of the students were recent arrivals in America with rich Talmudic and Hebraic knowledge, acquired in the leading European *Yeshivot,* who quickly mastered the requirements for college entrance as well as the college degree. And in addition to this heavy curriculum, I also had to take courses at Columbia to fulfil the arrangements I had made with Professor Schechter. But I enjoyed those four years and was thrilled to sit at the feet of the master scholars and teachers who were then acquiring a world-wide reputation for their contributions to Jewish learning.

A number of these professors were as yet new to the English language, and I must confess that it took many of the students—especially me—some time before we could easily follow the lectures of the sainted Professor Ginzberg and Professor Marx, both of whom then spoke with a heavy German accent. But to sit in the presence of the picturesque Professor Schechter and his colleagues made you feel that you were sitting before the great heads of the ancient Babylonian and Palestinian academies of learning.

Whenever I visited my parental home, father of course would question me on what I had learned, and when I repeated to him one of the brilliant Talmudic emendations or *halachic* interpretations of Professor Ginzberg, I could see the flash in his eyes which revealed his appreciation and admiration. Professor Schechter himself gave us a course in Jewish Theology, and how brilliantly he revealed the true essence of the classic rabbinic teachings!

In addition to the previously mentioned scholars, and the sainted Israel Davidson, who was then just beginning his teaching career, I was also privileged to sit at the feet of the unforgettable Israel Friedlander, who later met the death of a martyr in rendering help to our brethren in Russia. All of these men are well known to every intelligent Jew of our day. I had another teacher who, because he was not in the technical field of scholarship but only an officiating rabbi, is, alas, not so well known as he deserves. He was Rabbi Joseph Mayer Asher, our Professor in Homiletics, who died at the early age of 38, when I was in my senior year. I was greatly attached to him. He was handsome in appearance and spoke with eloquence. As a preacher he was remarkable, combining rich Jewish content with oratorical skill. He put his soul into his preaching, and you would see him physically exhausted at the conclusion of every sermon he delivered. Indeed, it was this steady, physical and nervous energy which he put into his preaching that brought on his untimely death.

Professor Asher was an enthusiastic disciple of the scholarly rabbi, Dr. Adolf Yellinek of Vienna, the greatest preacher of his age, who may rightfully be termed the father of the modern, truly Jewish sermon. The name and sermons of Yellinek were held before our eyes in almost every lecture. Because the student body then was very small, every student had to deliver at least one sermon in the Seminary Synagogue in each of the four years of study. On the Wednesday afternoon previous to the assigned Sabbath, the student preacher would offer his sermon before the entire school meeting in the auditorium by way of rehearsal and also to receive critical advice from the students and the professor. At each of these practice sessions Professor Schechter too was present. He laid much emphasis on the role of preaching, and foresaw the important influence that the preacher would exert in the modern synagogue. Though he himself was far removed from the art of oratory, it was interesting to see how carefully he noted not only faults in content but also in delivery. His presence at these sessions added the stamp of scholarly prestige which the sermon should deserve.

Professor Asher's death was a great blow not only to our student body but also to the entire American rabbinate because his method of preaching was making an impression upon many of the rabbis of both the old and the new schools. Professor Schechter appointed in that year a young and brilliant alumnus of the Seminary—Mordecai M. Kaplan—to become Dr. Asher's successor as Professor of Homiletics, a position which he held until recent years. As I was finishing my senior year at the time of his appointment, I was privileged to be his student in the homiletics class for only a very brief time; but already we, the students, foresaw the great career that was to be his.

Whenever I come to the Seminary I think how blessedly privileged the present students are to have the comforts of the magnificent and spacious dormitory building and dining room which they now enjoy. What hardships the out-of-town students encountered in my day! In my first year I was fortunate to have dear family friends in the Bronx with whom I could have home comforts. But it was a long and difficult subway ride from that neighborhood to the Seminary. In my second year I took a furnished room jointly with another Philadelphia student in a house close to the Seminary, but the problem of eating remained.

*　　*　　*

It was while I was still a student at the Seminary in New York that I married. The wedding was at my bride's home on South Broad Street, in Philadelphia, and the ceremony was performed by four rabbis—my sainted father, of blessed memory; Dr. Julius Greenstone, the minister of the Portuguese Synagogue, Mikveh Israel, and one of the early graduates of the Seminary; Dr. Bernard Revel, who lived in our home and was practically a member of our household; and a Rabbi Peikes, of New York. My bride and I returned to New York immediately after the wedding, as I had to take two examinations the very next day in courses which I took at the Summer School of Columbia. After the exams, we were able to take a brief honeymoon trip to Hunter, then a popular Jewish resort in the Catskills. We stayed at the Grand Hotel, where Professor Schechter, Professor Marx, their families, and a number of other Seminary teachers and students spent their vacation. It was good to be close to these wonderful people, who took us warmly to their hearts.

Upon our return to the city, we went immediately to the apartment which we had prepared before our marriage. It was a modest dwelling, a block away from the Seminary, on the fifth floor of a walk-up building on 122nd Street, near Broadway. My marriage was a daring step on my part because, unlike these days, when so many of the student body are married, all the students then, except one, were single. The one exception, popularly known as Pop Goldberg, was already a mature family man when he entered the Seminary.

In fact, everyone—family, friends, and even Professor Schechter—thought that my marrying at such an early age—I was only twenty—meant the end of my planned career. But they were mistaken; I was able to study with much more ease, and I did so with even greater zeal. It was hard on my wife, for she was a stranger in New York, away from all family and girlhood friends. And whenever I wanted to talk to her and to give her some time to offset her loneliness, she insisted that I spend that time in study—for she knew the predictions that had been made, and she, as well as I, wished to prove they were wrong. Many of the students, however, did appreciate the fact that one of their group had a home which they could visit.

I was also daring to marry for the simple reason that my financial resources were very meagre. I had had a position to preach bi-weekly on Friday nights and to take care of the Sunday School, during my first two student years, in the Wyona Street Temple, a very small congregation in the East New York section of Brooklyn; and after my marriage I succeeded in getting a week-end position in a little larger congregation on Noble Street, in the Greenpoint section, also in Brooklyn. The monthly pay offered in both of these positions was so nominal that the students of today would regard it as unworthy even of consideration. I also taught several afternoons in the week at the Hebrew School of the Hebrew Orphan Asylum in upper Manhattan, the principal of which in those years was Professor Israel Davidson.

We had little money, but we managed very well— or rather, I should say, Mrs. Levinthal managed very well—and our happiness was supreme. We had little time and little opportunity for diversion. On Saturday afternoons, however, a number of the students would visit us and enjoy the tea, fruit and crackers which "the Mrs.", as Mrs. Levinthal was called, served. Once in two or three weeks, we would really indulge in a treat.

On 125th Street there was the West End theatre, where many of the leading plays would start their road tours after finishing on Broadway. Tickets for the gallery were twenty-five cents. After dinner I would stand in line to get the choice seats, and Mrs. Levinthal, having completed her after-dinner chores, would meet me, and together we would climb the many flights of stairs to the gallery. After the show we would buy for a few pennies something special— like Swiss cheese—for a snack at home. I doubt that the young couples today who go to the smart cafes or supper clubs after the theatre enjoy themselves half as much as we did on those eventful evenings.

In certain weeks, when special occasion called for it, we treated ourselves more lavishly. I recall one week when E. H. Sothern and Julia Marlowe gave a repertoire of several Shakespearean plays, and we actually went to see three performances in one week. We made up the budget, however, by denying ourselves several other weeks' performances. As I think of the way we youngsters found contentment and happiness then, I can, in all truth say: "That, too, is a world gone by"—though I may add, again in utter truth, that even in those early days our regimen was not that of many other couples.

* * *

A month or two before my graduation, I was elected to my first regular position, Congregation B'nai Shalom, known as the Ninth Street Temple, in Brooklyn. The number of congregations in the entire country available for Seminary graduates was very few. In the entire borough of Brooklyn there were only two other congregations, and all three were quite small in membership and influence.

Throughout the country there were merely a few cities in which Seminary men were serving. Reform was then in its ascendency, and the richer Jews who sought social position, or who outgrew the East European environment which the old, orthodox synagogues retained, became members of the Reform Temples. As a matter of fact, a number of these congregations, served by Seminary men, which were already influential in those days, were offshoots of originally Reform congregations because they had rebelled at the extremes to which Reform was going. The membership of these were still made up largely of German Jews. The East European Jews were just beginning to think of the need for certain innovations that would make Synagogue worship attractive to the younger generation.

Graduates of the Seminary at that time could therefore not be selective in the choice of position as the graduates can be today. The salaries were pitifully low—my annual stipend during the entire five years that I served B'nai Shalom was $1500. And while the purchasing value of the dollar was far larger than it is today, this salary was hardly enough to meet the barest needs of a family. The smallest of the Reform congregations paid more than double that amount, and the larger ones paid salaries which could compare favorably with many offered today. The perquisites which the Seminary rabbi could expect for officiating at special occasions were also extremely modest. The average wedding fee was five dollars. It was customary for the rabbi to don a Prince Albert coat and to wear a high silk-hat, then called a "stove-pipe." Garbed in this fashion, I would ride to the wedding hall in the street car, for it would have been reckless extravagance to spend part of that fee on a taxicab.

No wonder there were so few young men who applied for admission to the Seminary. And yet, these very hardships had their advantages. The rabbinate was then a calling, not a profession, and the men who entered the Seminary did so despite the awareness that their career meant struggle and sacrifice; they felt an inward call to serve in this fashion their people and their God.

My installation as rabbi of my first regular position, as noted above, was celebrated in fine fashion. A rich program had been arranged in which the sainted Professor Friedlander, representing the Seminary, the renowned Rev. Masliansky, and my father, participated. I recall that after the meeting one of the officers, congratulating father, said to him: "Your son seems to be a fine rabbi, but he is so young." Father, evidently quick in evaluating the congregation, replied in Yiddish: *"Ich hob moiro az bei euch vet er gich alt veren"*—"I'm afraid that here he will age soon enough."

His evaluation proved correct. Not that I blame those people altogether: they were a product of the times. The Jews knew that they had to have a synagogue, but what the functions of the synagogue ought to be they did not realize. They felt that they ought to have a rabbi, but what his functions were to be was altogether unclear to them. I came aglow with the power of the sermon to teach and to inspire, and worked for many days in its preparation, but I soon discovered that that was not what they wanted. More than anything else, the rabbi was expected to be a solicitor for new members—a go-getter for funds among the shop-keepers in the neighborhood.

My task became all the more difficult, since I succeeded a free-lance, so-called rabbi, a glib talker, who had told humorous stories from the pulpit to entertain the congregation and had visited his members frequently to join them in card playing. Every cultural effort which I tried to sponsor was met with indifference. There were a few enlightened Jews who tried to help me but they, too, were helpless. So far as religious needs were concerned, this was the generation of the wilderness.

*   *   *

A deep despair overtook me. No other position was open which I could consider, and I finally decided to take up law. Unknown to anyone except my wife, I studied law for three years, receiving the Doctor Juris degree from New York University in 1914. I can state in all sincerity that this added course did not diminish in any way my attention to all my congregational duties. It did mean three years of tremendously exhausting work. Strange as it may seem, practically everyone in the congregation was happy to learn the news of my graduation when it was reported in the newspapers, and they felt that I had taken a wise step. Somehow, they also felt that it was a pity for me to waste my efforts on such a hopeless cause as religion. In fact, one of the officers—a successful lawyer—invited me to become associated in his office on terms most generous and favorable to me, and the congregation, also desirous to be helpful, allowed me to accept the offer and at the same time continue my ministerial work for it.

I passed the bar examinations the following month and was soon formally licensed as a counselor and attorney-at-law. Clients began to call on me much sooner than I had anticipated. I tried a number of cases in the lower courts and within a few months won an important case in the Supreme Court. In six months my income was larger than my annual rabbinic salary—as if the Satan of economic success was determined to alienate me more and more from the ambition of my youth.

But I was far from happy. I enjoyed the study of law; the cases and the judicial decisions which we had to read fascinated me and reminded me so much of the method of Talmudic jurisprudence. But I could not accommodate myself to the practice of the law, and my heart yearned for a complete devotion to rabbinical work. It was my good fortune that the heavenly guiding angel who had seemed so often to be helpful to me in the past did not forsake me now.

*   *   *

Just about that time, a group of the most prominent and successful Jews in the thickly populated Jewish section of Brooklyn known as Brownsville banded together for the purpose of organizing a modern congregation which would be faithful to Jewish tradition and at the same time adopt those innovations which were beginning to be recognized by the more Americanized Jews as essential for the modern synagogue. They erected a fine synagogue building in the new Eastern Parkway section, to which the wealthier Jews of the Brownsville and the Williamsburg sections were moving.

Among this founding group were two men, Victor Schwartz and Moses Bernstein, very active and popular in the Zionist movement. They had followed my Zionist interest and activities not only in Brooklyn but also on the national scene. At the famous Zionist Convention in 1915, held in Boston, at which Justice Louis D. Brandeis made his first public appearance in the role of Zionist leader, I had occasion to speak during a number of the discussion sessions. These two gentlemen then informed me of the new synagogue project in which they were vitally interested, and asked me whether I would permit them to suggest my name to the officers then considering engaging a rabbi. Such permission I readily granted. They must have acted quickly, because while still in Boston I received an invitation from the Principal of Public School 84 in Brownsville to deliver the main address at the school graduation exercises to be held within the coming week.

The president of the newly formed congregation, William B. Roth, the manager of the leading bank in that section, was a member of the local School Board, and he evidently had planned this invitation so that he and a few of the leaders could meet me and hear me speak. I delivered the address and must have made a good impression because the president not only congratulated me but also insisted that I accompany him to his office immediately after the exercises. The position was then and there offered to me, and without discussing any terms whatsoever I accepted and became the Rabbi of Temple Petach Tikvah, a name which the two Zionist leaders had proposed.

I instantly saw the fine possibilities for effective Jewish work through this Temple. In all that seething mass of Jews which then inhabited Brownsville there was not one synagogue which had an English-speaking rabbi. The young people, students of high school and college, had no opportunity to hear a Jewish message presented to them in the language and manner which they could appreciate. Many of these young people flocked to the Labor Lyceum, which conducted a public forum where leading economic and social leaders spoke, and where the liberal Christian minister, John Haynes Holmes, also participated, but no specifically Jewish themes—particularly religious—were included in the programs. There had already been established the Hebrew Educational Society, at which lectures on Jewish historic and cultural themes were given, but religion had a small part in its early programs.

I recall that I had accepted the Temple position without even discussing terms. A week or two later I received an invitation to visit the president at his home to discuss further plans with the officers. I presented a very ambitious program of Temple activities which greatly interested them, and the enthusiasm at this conference was high.

Suddenly, the president turned to me and reminded me that they had not as yet talked about salary. "Rabbi, what is your request?" he asked. Without giving any thought to the matter, and realizing that I was dealing with a much more prosperous group than I had in South Brooklyn, I replied: "I leave this matter entirely to you, and will abide by your judgment." The president, a very cultured Jew who in his youth had attended a Hungarian Yeshiva and who had developed into a successful banker in America, immediately countered with the question: "What salary do you receive in your present congregation?" "Fifteen hundred dollars," I naively replied, without adding that its members were chiefly shopkeepers and white-collar people to whom even this sum represented a sacrifice. "If that is the case, we will give you $1800," was his immediate reply.

I must confess that at the moment I felt a keen disappointment. For while I had not expected a much larger salary, I had thought that these men, all of them quite wealthy, would want the rabbi to live in fair comfort. But I answered: "I said that I would leave it to your judgment, and I stand by my first reply!"

*   *   *

On relating this incident later to my colleagues, I was criticized for permitting these people to take advantage of me. And yet I never regretted this agreement. My great reward was the remarkable success of all my work at this Temple. A Friday night service, which I instituted immediately on my assumption of duties, was a novelty for the Brownsville and Eastern Parkway Jews, and, long before the announced hour for the service, standing room only greeted the men and women who flocked to the Temple from every part of that section of Brooklyn.

The leading families occupied the front pews and were faithful in their attendance. Every Friday night was a festive occasion; the women came dressed in the best of fashion, and the officers, trustees and other leading workers would come wearing frock coats and high hats. The Temple, its school and its activities became the main topic of discussion among all classes of Brownsville Jewry.

What a different Jewish life I faced! I was happy to give up the law and to devote all my time and energy to this work which was so close to my heart. The work was difficult and time-consuming, for in those years the rabbi had to do everything alone; and throughout the four and one-half years that I was at Petach Tikvah, and for at least the first fifteen or twenty years at the Brooklyn Jewish Center, I had not only to preach sermons both at the Friday night and the Sabbath morning services, but also to act as principal of the daily Hebrew School, to direct the youth club activities and to supervise all the cultural and religious programs of the affiliate organizations. There was little time for myself, and yet, despite it all, I revelled in the work and was grateful to God that I could return in such happy circumstances to the love of my youth—the Rabbinate.

*   *   *

After the first three years at Petach Tikvah, however, something occurred that changed the friendly atmosphere there and eventually brought an important change in my life, too. The Jewish community in the entire borough of Brooklyn showed a remarkable growth in population, in influence and in the realization of its Jewish needs. Being by nature very community-minded, I naturally threw myself into all the larger communal efforts. Believing, too, that the Synagogue's function was not only to serve the religious needs of those affiliated with it but also to help inspire, direct and become the center of community needs, I strove to make Petach Tikvah an influential factor in the promotion and development of all communal endeavors. The president of the Temple, who, as I already noted, was in many respects an unusually interesting personality and who had shown me many evidences of real friendship and admiration, suddenly began to resent my community activities as well as the activities in this field of many of the Temple's leading members.

Brooklyn Jewry was then in the process of awakening and self-discovery. The Federation of Jewish Charities, which until then had represented a small group of influential German Jews, was beginning to win many East European Jews who became well known for their Jewish interests. The Zionist movement underwent a resurgence in every part of Brooklyn, and I saw to it that the membership of my congregation should play an active and leading role in it. My president, however, had an altogether different concept of the functions of the rabbi and of the synagogue. The rabbi's interests, he felt, should be limited to the synagogue and its own program of activities; the members' interests should not be diverted from the needs of the synagogue, and the function of the synagogue had to remain confined to its own limited program. A clash thus arose as to the fundamental philosophy of the function of the rabbi and the synagogue, and the clash grew stronger with every passing day.

*   *   *

About that time, in 1918, a group of Jews on the West Side of Manhattan, friends and followers of Professor Mordecai M. Kaplan, began to put into effect a project which he had been the first to propose—the building of a Synagogue Center which would in itself provide for all the individual Jew's needs—religious, cultural, social, even physical— and at the same time become the center of activity in behalf of all Jewish needs. A number of the leading members of Petach Tikvah were attracted to this new concept of the Synagogue.

It so happened that a brother of the president of this New York Jewish Center lived in the Eastern Parkway section, but he was not a member of Petach Tikvah. He kept bringing to his friends in our section daily reports of the progress of the New York project, and thus the idea took root among many of my people in Petach Tikvah, as well as among a number of the new arrivals in our neighborhood who had not yet joined any congregation, to found a similar institution. This resulted in the formal organization of the Brooklyn Jewish Center, which was incorporated early in 1919.

In the fall of that year a committee of the leading sponsors of this new movement called at my home to extend to me the call to become their first rabbi. I pleaded with them to postpone this invitation until they were more advanced in the furtherance of their plans and until they were more assured of community support. But they were insistent that I join them then, for, as they were frank to assure me, my leadership would help their efforts. I therefore accepted the call, and on a Friday night in October, 1919 I preached my farewell sermon at Petach Tikvah. It was with a heart full of sadness, and with a mind of fondest memories, that I faced the congregation that Sabbath eve, but I was comforted by the thought that I was remaining in the neighborhood and that I would be able to continue my personal friendship with most of the members. Indeed, for almost the remainder of the year I worshipped at the Temple as a congregant, for the Center had no place yet for worship but only an office in which it conducted its meetings and congregational, organization affairs.

It was once more a daring step which I had taken. The group that I joined was very small, consisting of not more than twenty-five men. When they extended to me their call, they had nothing tangible to show but only a beautiful dream and great enthusiasm. They had no definite plans for the building they proposed to erect. They did have some encouraging pledges of financial support, but they were not at all certain that the Center idea would appeal to many Jews. But I had complete faith in the success of the venture, and I had constant proof that my faith was not misplaced. I did little actual work for them that year, merely helping the group to plan and develop a program for future activities.

I utilized that year in pursuing special studies at the Seminary and in writing my thesis for the degree of Doctor of Hebrew Literature, which I was awarded at the graduation exercises in June, 1920. I took this post-graduate work under the aegis of Professor Ginzberg, and my law studies were of much help to me, for the subject of the thesis which Professor Ginzberg had suggested to me was "The Jewish Law of Agency—With Special Reference to the Roman and Common Law."

*   *   *

I was happy and grateful for this opportunity to advance, in intensive fashion, my Jewish studies, for I realized how great would be the demands on my time once the Center was built.

The new institution to which I now joined my life caught the imagination of all types of Jews— those who had been brought up in the old, strict observance of tradition and those who were already alienated from all Jewish religious life; and yet, we succeeded in making the Synagogue the most attractive and most influential phase of all our activities. The membership far outgrew the most hopeful dreams of the founders, and the institution immediately became the center of the widespread interests of Brooklyn's growing Jewry. It became, too, the pioneer of a new and healthful evolution of the concept of the synagogue throughout the country, and thus was the primary influence in the organization and establishment of Synagogue Centers in every section of the land.

*   *   *

I have now come to an era of Jewish life well familiar to most Jews of our day, and reminiscences are no longer in order. I have tried to record memories of a world that has truly passed, a world in which Jewish life in America was being moulded and transformed from the East European style into an American pattern. The wise author of Ecclesiastes tells us: "A generation goeth and a generation cometh, but the world endureth forever." [7] I have witnessed the passing of a generation and the com-

---

7. Ecclesiastes, 1 :4.

ing of a new generation in American Jewry, and I am all the more convinced that the world of Jewish life will endure.

Just as every Jewish generation in the past several thousand years left its mark upon the growth and development of Judaism and preserved and strengthened its future, so too, I feel assured, the new generation now on the American scene will make its beneficial contribution to Jewish thought and practice and thereby prove once more that the world of Jewish living endureth forever.

THE AUTHOR

The author is Rabbi of the Brooklyn Jewish Center, one of the most influential congregations in the country and one of the first to develop the Synagogue Center idea, the new concept of the role of the Synagogue in modern life. He has served it since its founding in 1919.

He was Visiting Professor of Homiletics at the Jewish Theological Seminary of America from 1947 to 1962.

Rabbi Levinthal is descended on both paternal and maternal sides from a long list of distinguished Rabbis—traced back through more than a dozen generations.

He has been President of the Rabbinical Assembly of America; first President of the Brooklyn Board of Rabbis; first President of the Brooklyn Jewish Community Council; Trustee of the Israel Matz Foundation for Hebrew Writers; and one of the leaders of the Zionist Organization of America and the United Synagogue of America.

In addition to having the degrees of J.D. and L.H.D., in course, Rabbi Levinthal is the recipient of two honorary degrees—Doctor of Divinity from the Jewish Theological Seminary, and Doctor of Jewish Theology from the Jewish Institute of Religion.